T0286806

Cambridge Elements ≡

Elements in Ancient Egypt in Context
edited by
Gianluca Miniaci
University of Pisa
Juan Carlos Moreno García
CNRS Paris
Anna Stevens
University of Cambridge and Monash University

FAMINE AND FEAST
IN ANCIENT EGYPT

Ellen Morris
Barnard College, Columbia University

CAMBRIDGE
UNIVERSITY PRESS

Shaftesbury Road, Cambridge CB2 8EA, United Kingdom

One Liberty Plaza, 20th Floor, New York, NY 10006, USA

477 Williamstown Road, Port Melbourne, VIC 3207, Australia

314–321, 3rd Floor, Plot 3, Splendor Forum, Jasola District Centre, New Delhi – 110025, India

103 Penang Road, #05–06/07, Visioncrest Commercial, Singapore 238467

Cambridge University Press is part of Cambridge University Press & Assessment, a department of the University of Cambridge.

We share the University's mission to contribute to society through the pursuit of education, learning and research at the highest international levels of excellence.

www.cambridge.org
Information on this title: www.cambridge.org/9781009074582

DOI: 10.1017/9781009070713

First published 2023

A catalogue record for this publication is available from the British Library.

ISBN 978-1-009-07458-2 Paperback
ISSN 2516-4813 (online)
ISSN 2516-4805 (print)

Famine and Feast in Ancient Egypt

Elements in Ancient Egypt in Context

DOI: 10.1017/9781009070713
First published online: June 2023

Ellen Morris
Barnard College, Columbia University
Author for correspondence: Ellen Morris, efm2110@columbia.edu

Abstract: This Element is about the creation and curation of social memory in pharaonic and Greco-Roman Egypt. Ancient, Classical, Medieval, and Ottoman sources attest to the horror that characterized catastrophic famines. Occurring infrequently and rarely reaching the canonical seven-years' length, famines appeared and disappeared like nightmares. Communities that remain aware of potentially recurring tragedies are often advantaged in their efforts to avert or ameliorate worst-case scenarios. For this and other reasons, pharaonic and Greco-Roman Egyptians preserved intergenerational memories of hunger and suffering. This Element begins with a consideration of the trajectories typical of severe Nilotic famines and the concept of social memory. It then argues that personal reflection and literature, prophecy, and an annual festival of remembrance functioned – at different times, and with varying degrees of success – to convince the well-fed that famines had the power to unseat established order and to render a comfortably familiar world unrecognizable.

Keywords: famine, festival, literature, prophecy, memory

ISBNs: 9781009074582 (PB), 9781009070713 (OC)
ISSNs: 2516-4813 (online), 2516-4805 (print)

Contents

1 Famine and Social Memory

It is hard to imagine that the passage of a century largely erased the flu pandemic of 1918–1920 from the memories of all but historians and epidemiologists. Such was the case until early in 2020. Suddenly, another highly contagious disease began to turn lives across the globe upside down. Photographs and stories from the 1918 pandemic, newly excavated from archives, quickly went viral (Figure 1). As in a distant mirror, masked women and men queued in long lines for basic supplies or stepped up to triage victims. The unmasked assembled to protest public health mandates. Businesses closed, the infected were quarantined, hospitals filled and then spilled over, and dead bodies exceeded the storage capacities of morgues.

Some disasters, although they could (and should) have been predicted, take those who experience them by surprise. Others, however, may be pessimistically awaited. This Element explores the reasons – many of them surprising – why even during peace and prosperity, ancient Egyptians *expected* social upheaval and tragedy. Specifically, it argues that in pharaonic and Greco-Roman Egypt infrequent but devastating episodes of famine remained in social memory by virtue of three mnemonic media: witness testimony and literature, prophecy, and rites of remembrance. By writing, warning, and revisiting, Egyptians kept the memory of terrible famines fresh, even when no one alive had experienced anything comparable.

This section has two aims. First, it sets the stakes of the arguments in this Element by describing the consequences of extended Nile flood failure. To do so, it draws on pharaonic and Greco-Roman documents as well as richly detailed Medieval and Ottoman accounts that collectively illuminate the typical trajectory of Egypt's most harrowing famines. The section's second aim is to consider how individual memories of communal tragedies are transmitted into social memory. As with viral epidemics, the speed and efficiency with which preventative measures are put into place at the onset of a food crisis can potentially forestall mass mortality. For the urgency of their implementation to be appreciated, however, extreme hunger must be recalled by a population that has never seen the corrosive effects of starvation on a body, much less on the body politic.

The three remaining sections focus on mechanisms that preserved such memories. Section 2 addresses the attempts of individuals – via personal narratives or imaginative recreations – to convey the experience of living through a period of famine in all its attendant turmoil and terror. Section 3 examines the framing of famine as a manifestation of divine displeasure. The authors of Greco-Roman prophetic texts drew frequently and vividly upon the specter of famine for their own political purposes. Even when the calamity they "foresaw" was already happening, their prophecies often circulated widely and kept the consequences of environmental catastrophe alive in the imagination of later

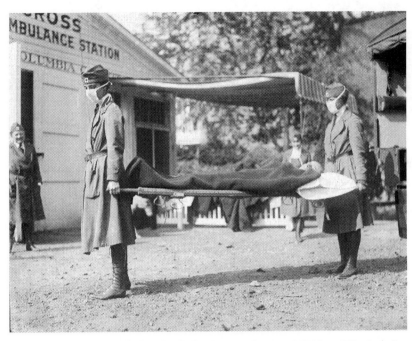

Figure 1 Ambulance during the influenza pandemic of 1918, public domain.
Accessed from LOC's public domain archive

(Red cross emergency ambulance in the influenza pandemic of 1918. https://loc
.getarchive.net/media/demonstration-at-the-red-cross-emergency-ambulance-station-in-
washington-dc-a3af7c Open source)

generations. The final section focuses on what may well have been the most
successful strategy, the transformation and incorporation of past, but potentially
recurrent, traumas into ritual. Visions of a world turned upside down invoked in
festival settings dramatize revolutions in social status that occur as a result of
famines, insurrections, and wars. At the same time, they serve as enduring and
thought-provoking sources of delight. The ancient Egyptian New Year's Festival,
discussed in this section, offered a sobering annual reminder of the very real
possibility of famine. Egyptians eagerly awaited the opportunity to remember,
however, as they were invited to drink until drunkenness, to transgress sexual
boundaries, and to enjoy festive inversions that both educated and amused them.

1.1 Severe Nile Failures Occurred Rarely but Followed
a Predictable Pattern

Prior to the construction of the Aswan Dam, Egypt's predominantly agricultural
economy was dependent on an annual inundation that was neither too high nor
too low (Figure 2). A flood of 9 m or more would leave fields under water at

Figure 2 The Nile inundation near the pyramids, c. 1930s, public domain. Accessed from Mena House Hotel Pinterest

sowing time and cause widespread damage to homes, granaries, and agricultural infrastructure. A flood of 6.7 m was both average and benevolent, but a crest that failed to attain 5.3 m caused great concern (Bell 1971: 6; Seidlmayer 2001: 33–6). In his *Natural History*, Pliny wrote:

> Its most desirable height is sixteen cubits; if the waters do not attain that height, the overflow is not universal; but if they exceed that measure, by their slowness in receding they tend to delay the process of cultivation. In the latter case the time for sowing is lost, in consequence of the moisture of the soil; in the former, the ground is so parched that the seed-time comes to no purpose . . . . When the water rises to only twelve cubits, it experiences the horrors of famine; when it attains thirteen, hunger is still the result; a rise of fourteen cubits is productive of gladness; a rise of fifteen sets all anxieties at rest; while an increase of sixteen is productive of unbounded transports of joy. (Plin. *Nat.* 5.10.3)

Vespasian was so delighted by the sixteen cubits the Nile purportedly rose during his period of residency in Alexandria – tangible proof of his popularity with the gods – that he commissioned a statue of the personified Nile deity surrounded by sixteen plump little toddlers for his Temple of Peace in Rome (Henrichs 1968: 73–4). Similarly, Egyptians in the thirteenth century referred to an auspicious sixteen-cubit flood as "sultan's water" (al-Baghdādi 1965: 50 *l*).

A good flood was not to be taken for granted: between the seventh and fifteenth centuries CE only 73 percent of the recorded heights would have brought cheer, security, or prosperity. As many as 12 percent likely occasioned great alarm (Gnirs 2015: 109). From the dawn of the state, if not before, Nilometers were developed to measure the height of the inundation. The first annals in Egyptian history arose from such records, and it is significant that one of the initiatory acts of Christian supremacy in Egypt was to remove the sacred cubit rod from the temple of Serapis and rededicate it to Christ in the church of Alexandria (Socrates Scholasticus, *Historia Ecclesiastica* 1.18). The height of the inundation allowed the state to predict taxation revenue, just as, in the case of worrisome results, it prompted the institution of austerity measures.

The letters of the farmer and funerary priest Heqanakht, which date to the reign of Senwosret I (c. 1920–1875) at the beginning of the Twelfth Dynasty, are illustrative in this regard. In one letter Heqanakht wrote to his family while executing responsibilities far from home at a time when the Nile's rise had been worrisomely low. Just as expressions of concern became *de rigueur* in the first few lines of an email written at the onset of the coronavirus pandemic, Heqanakht's letter begins by reassuring his family that he is, in fact, alive. He then responds to complaints he received (or expected to receive) about the strict rations he had imposed on his dependents, chiding,

> Look, you are that one who ate to his satisfaction when he was hungry to the white of his eyes. Look, the whole land is dead and [you] have not hungered. Look, before I came upstream here, I made your salaries to perfection. [Now], has the inundation been very [big]? Look, [our] salary has been made for us according to the state of the inundation, which one and all bear. Look, I have managed to keep you alive so far. (Allen 2002: 16)

Records from Medieval and Ottoman times indicate that the potentially disastrous effects of insufficient or overabundant floods were most often mitigated by imposing strict rations, distributing grain from government granaries and the stores of wealthy citizens, importing grain from unaffected areas, and punishing profiteers (Sabra 2000: 136–66). Through such anticipatory measures and careful attention to agricultural infrastructure, low floods brought concern far more often than catastrophe.

Famines that caused mass mortality tended to occur mainly when low floods clustered in time, occurred in conjunction with a region-wide drought, and/or were exacerbated by an inefficient, corrupt, or entirely absent central government. Both Strabo (*Geography* 17.1.3) and Napoleon (de Montholon 1847: 213) correlated satisfactory flood management with strong governance, yet each failed to appreciate the potential power that a series of erratic floods possessed to widen preexisting fault lines and transform a functioning regime into one racked with insurgency and revolt.

Scientific research into the effect of significant shifts in climate and monsoon patterns on the ecology of the Nile Valley has accelerated within the last fifteen years, leaving little doubt that at certain periods in Egypt's history dangerous floods and droughts combined to render life unusually precarious for pastoralists and agriculturalists alike (cf. studies summarized in Manning 2018: 95–9, 135–72; Creasman 2020; and Section 2) For the pharaonic period, the Old and New Kingdoms faltered and ultimately failed at the onset of extended climatic downturns (lasting from c. 2200–1900 and 1200–850, respectively). Prolonged periods during which agricultural surpluses could not be counted upon undoubtedly hampered the efforts of aggrandizers to reconstitute a central government. While weather fluctuated within these periods, and explanations for state failure are complex, texts written in both eras are anomalous in their repeated references to hunger, large-scale population movements, and unrest. So too, multiple volcanic eruptions that occurred while Egypt was under Ptolemaic rule have been shown with 98 percent certainty to have significantly reduced Nile flooding. Indeed, "eight of the nine documented periods of social unrest occurred within a narrow window of these eruptions" (Manning 2018: 136). Famines in the mid-third century CE once again demonstrated that climatic and social change went hand in hand (Harper 2017: 131–4). Toleration of institutionalized social inequality, it seems, plummets in times of hunger.

Prior to modern large-scale hydraulic engineering, severe Nilotic famines conformed to a broadly predictable trajectory.[1] Drought frequently preceded the failure of the inundation and caused an influx of climate refugees and a corresponding uptick in xenophobia – a harbinger of trouble that unfortunately feels very familiar today. When the floods failed or became overly abundant, the price of grain skyrocketed in anticipation of scarcity. As a result, even in advance of the famine, and certainly during it, profiteering ran rampant, bread riots erupted, people congregated in protest, and government infrastructure came under attack.

As the situation worsened, it was common for people to resort to banditry, larceny, and murder. The more desperate the food shortage became, the more people began to exploit starvation food (unripe beans, cats, garbage, etc.). Social bonds that had strengthened at the beginning of the crisis began to break down, even within families. Unthinkable acts such as infanticide or even cannibalism occurred (or were said to occur), and people progressively abandoned hope for help from either men or gods (Figure 3). Finally, due to

---

[1] References pertinent to the stages of famine in Egypt listed below may be found in Morris 2019: 79–83; 2020: 235–43. See too, al-Maqrīzī 1994: 27–49; Hassan 1997: 10–17; Mikhail 2011: 217–18.

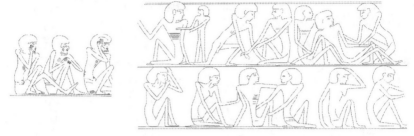

Figure 3 Scenes of starving Bedouin from the causeways of the Fifth
Dynasty kings Sahure (left) and Unas (right) (redrawn after Hawass and
Verner 1996: 185, figure 2a, with the kind permission of Z. Hawass;
Drioton 1943: 49, figure 3)

starvation and to weakened immune systems vulnerable to pestilence, body
counts soared, and burial rites no longer took place. In the end, there were too
many bodies to mourn or even to bury.

Accounts of six devastating, well-documented famines in Egypt over the
course of seven centuries should help demonstrate the degree to which the
narratives related by eyewitnesses and chroniclers constitute variations on
a single terrifying theme. The deeds that survivors of each of these famines
witnessed – or perhaps even resorted to – must have ensured that they suffered
from post-traumatic stress long after the natural world had righted itself.

1.1.1 1064–1071

A seven-year famine brought about by low Nile floods under the watch of a weak
state led to unrest among Bedouin, rampant inflation, an epidemic, and such
a dramatic depopulation of the countryside that even areas that had been flooded
were left uncultivated. Travel was impossible without a large escort, and prices rose
so high that a rich woman purportedly couldn't sell a thousand-dinar necklace for
flour. The chief dignitary in Egypt was said to have sold everything in his palace
and robbed the tombs of his ancestors to purchase food. Commoners resorted to
eating dogs, cats, and (eventually) other people (al-Maqrīzī 1994: 37–38).

1.1.2 1199–1201

After a low Nile, prices began to rise. According to ʿAbd al-Latif al-Baghdādi,
who witnessed the famine,

> The provinces were made desolate by drought; the inhabitants foresaw an inevit-
> able scarcity, and the dread of the famine excited tumultuous movements among
> them. The inhabitants of villages and of the country districts retired to the
> principal towns of the provinces .... There was also an infinite multitude who

sought a retreat in the towns of Misr and Cairo, where they suffered an appalling
famine and a frightful mortality . . . . [T]he plague and contagion began to make
itself felt, and the poor, pressed by the famine which struck them always, ate
carrion, corpses, dogs, and the excrement and the filth of the animals. This went
on a long time, until they began to eat little children. (al-Baghdādi 1965:
55 *l*–56 *r*)

According to al-Baghdādi, parents often consumed their own children, on the
assumption that it was better that they be eaten by a relative than by a stranger
(al-Baghdādi 1965: 56 *r*–56 *l*; 59 *l*). Cannibalism excited significantly less
commentary as the famine persisted.

1.1.3 1294–1296

Combined region-wide drought and Nile failures at the end of the thirteenth
century led fifty thousand or so Libyans to migrate to Egypt. Prices rose thirteen
times their normal level. People ate carrion, dogs, cats, and even the human
corpses that littered the streets. One chronicler witnessed outside the city gate of
Cairo a large group of people resembling "savage beasts who had lost any sign
of humanity," fighting with one another over the right to consume the corpses
deposited there (Sabra 2000: 141–3; Raphael 2013: 91).

1.1.4 1402–1404

Caused by a combination of low Niles and inept governance, the massive death
toll was exacerbated by plague. Certain elites were said to have provided burials
for one hundred to two hundred people per day. In the face of rampant inflation,
people migrated in search of grain, sold their children, and, purportedly in at
least one case, resorted to cannibalism (Sabra 2000: 152–3).

1.1.5 1694–1695

An insufficient flood led prices to rise. Thousands of peasants abandoned their
villages and fled to Cairo in search of food. Although the Ottoman government
lessened taxes and mandated that elites provision the poor, mobs stormed the
citadel of Cairo and looted granaries. When there was no more grain to beg or
steal, people consumed the corpses of cats and humans. The co-occurrence of the
plague and famine ensured that the dead were numerous (Mikhail 2011: 216–17).

1.1.6 1790–1796

The tragic events of this famine are especially interesting from an Egyptological
perspective, as they began with torrential rains and devastating flash floods,
such as appear to be preserved in geological strata dating to late in the reign of

Pepi II (c. 2200) at the very end of the Old Kingdom (Welc and Marks 2014: 131; Kuraszkiewicz 2016: 30, 32). Damage to houses, businesses, irrigation infrastructure, and grain storage installations meant that the following year's insufficient inundation brought severe famine. Suffering caused by the unusual downpours and drought made Egyptians of all social levels susceptible to a plague that killed the leader and many of his followers and caused a crisis, "as no appointed leader could stay alive long enough to rule effectively" (Mikhail 2011: 222). The onset of a drought in the fall of 1791 resulted in price hikes, revolts, and widespread migration to Cairo, which placed further stress on scant grain reserves and ensured that far fewer farmers remained to repair the dikes and till the soil in preparation for the next sowing season. Many thousands died, and those struggling to survive resorted to consuming the corpses of horses, donkeys, and finally children (Hassan 1997: 11; Mikhail 2008: 261–3, 268–72).

Attestations of cannibalism in primary sources are often met with justifiable skepticism by historians. Two contemporary statements from the long First Intermediate Period in Egypt (c. 2160–1895 BCE), for example, are roundly dismissed as hyperbole. Heqanakht, marshalling further justification for his tight rations, admonished his family to be grateful because "[h]alf of life is better than death in full. Look, one should say hunger (only) about (real) hunger. Look, they've started to eat people here" (Allen 2002: 17), while another witness, Ankhtifi of Mo'Alla, boasted of his ability to enlarge his territory, protect his people, and provide them with sustenance – even though elsewhere whole populations traveled upstream and downstream like locusts in search of food. "All of Upper Egypt was dying of hunger and people were eating their children," he noted, "but I did not allow anybody to die of hunger in this nome" (Seidlmayer 2000: 129). Because in both instances the purported cannibalism happened elsewhere, Egyptologists interpret the references as lurid and self-serving rhetorical flourishes.

Such evocations, however, are not staple fodder in famine narratives. The six examples listed earlier appear to be unique in Medieval and Ottoman Egypt, as cannibalism is not highlighted in accounts of the six other catastrophic famines for which good records survive (namely those of 963–971, 1372–1373, 1415–1416, 1449–1452, 1784–1787, and 1877–1879). So too, cannibalism was *never* attributed to situations that might more aptly be termed food crises than famines. While specialists in Chinese history have been similarly skeptical of references to cannibalism in their own historical records, a recent declassification by the Chinese government of documents pertaining to the Great Famine, which took place from 1958–1962, makes it clear that – as al-Baghdādī noted with respect to the famine he witnessed – cannibalism was widespread and alarmingly routine. Frank Dikötter, author of *Mao's Great Famine: The History of China's Most Devastating Catastrophe, 1958–1962,* writes of one such cache of documents:

> As the catastrophe unfolded, people were forced to resort to previously unthinkable acts to survive. As the moral fabric of society unraveled, they abused one another, stole from one another and poisoned one another. Sometimes they resorted to cannibalism. One police investigation from Feb. 25, 1960, details some 50 cases in Yaohejia village in Gansu: "Name of culprit: Yang Zhongsheng. Name of victim: Yang Ecshun. Relationship with culprit: younger brother. Manner of crime: killed and eaten. Reason: livelihood issues." (Dikötter 2010)

Distilled into the driest of crime reports, unthinkable acts appear in abundance, and this cache was no anomaly. Archival evidence suggests that "several thousand" such cases occurred over the course of these four years (Yang 2008: 524, n. 23). So too, during the worst of the two-and-a-half-year siege of Leningrad in World War II, roughly fifteen hundred of the city's inhabitants were arrested for cannibalism. Such acts were often perpetrated within families and on occasion to save the lives of children (Peri 2017: 107–8). Although this situation was unprecedented in living memory – and necessitated the creation of special divisions of police and psychiatrists – it was, perhaps, predictable. Famine historian Cormac Ó Gráda maintains that cannibalism should be considered one of the defining characteristics of severe famine (Ó Gráda 2015: 5).

As horrific as famines were, their misery was concentrated. Exceptionally severe episodes tended to be both brief and infrequent. Moreover, with few exceptions – as occurred in especially hard-hit centuries – catastrophic famines skipped multiple generations. Personal memories that are communicated orally and *only* orally, as studies have shown, cannot be retrieved more than eighty to a hundred years after an event occurred (Assmann 2006: 24). For this reason, mnemonic strategies that encode communal trauma into social memory are vital.

1.2 The Preservation of "Counterfactual" Social Memory Can Be Considered a Survival Strategy

Memories of "unforgettable" events are uniquely challenging to preserve and transmit. Friedrich Nietzsche and Sigmund Freud both believed that the memories most likely to lodge in the psyche of an individual – or even an ethnic group or a nation – would be the most painful (Assmann 2006: 3–6). In fact, however, events in which individuals commit and/or witness acts of cruelty and desperation plunge into obscurity by multiple means. Veterans and Holocaust survivors, for example, have been famously reluctant to speak of their

PHARAONIC AND GRECO-ROMAN CHRONOLOGY	
EARLY DYNASTIC PERIOD	**2900–2545**
Dynasty 1	2900–2730
Dynasty 2	2730–2590
OLD KINGDOM	**2592–2152**
Dynasty 3	2592–2544
Dynasty 4	2543–2436
Dynasty 5	2435–2306
Dynasty 6	2305–2118
FIRST INTERMEDIATE PERIOD	**2150–1980**
Dynasty 8	2150–2118
Dynasties 9 and 10 (Herakleopolitan)	2118–1980
Dynasty 11 (Theban)	2080–1980
MIDDLE KINGDOM	**1980–1760**
Dynasty 11 (All Egypt)	1980–1940
Dynasty 12	1939–1760
SECOND INTERMEDIATE PERIOD	**1759–c. 1539**
Dynasty 13	1759–c. 1630
Dynasty 14	?
Dynasty 15	?–c. 1530
Dynasties 16 and 17	?–1540
NEW KINGDOM	**1539–1077**
Dynasty 18	1539–1292
Dynasty 19	1292–1191
Dynasty 20	1190–1077
THIRD INTERMEDIATE PERIOD	**1076–723**
Dynasty 21	1076–944
Dynasty 22	943–c. 746
Dynasty 23–24	845–723
LATE PERIOD	**722–332**
Dynasty 25	722–c. 655
Dynasty 26	664–525
Dynasty 27	525–404
Dynasty 28	404–399
Dynasty 29	399–380
Dynasty 30	380–343
2nd Persian Period	343–332
PTOLEMAIC PERIOD	**332–30**
ROMAN PERIOD	**30 BCE–395 CE**

Figure 4 Chronological table (after Hornung, Krauss, and Warburton 2006: 490–5)

experiences to those that remain psychically unscarred. Additionally, studies have shown that the memories of those suffering from post-traumatic stress are often unreliable in certain respects and prone to repression (LaCapra 2014; van der Kolk 2015). Reluctance to speak often fades in old age, when individuals realize that memories of seemingly unspeakable events – and thus the lessons that could potentially aid their descendants – might remain forever untold. Yet as decade follows decade, memories shift and are often effaced (Ó Gráda 2001: 130–2).

Daily life – present both before and after tragedy – has a way of enveloping horrific events. Thus, in the aftermath of famine, the natural order reverts to a predictable normalcy. Emaciated bodies are no longer seen, demography

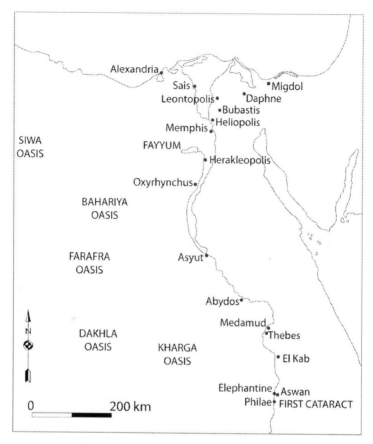

Figure 5 Map of Egypt with relevant sites

bounces back, and new generations are born into plenty. For a person who never experienced famine, then, to actively recall a societal memory of it necessitates introducing what Jan Assmann terms a "counterfactual element" into the present. Preserving counterfactual memory, he asserts, was a central project of texts like those in the Torah, where

> [t]he people are expected to master the trick of remembering privation in the midst of abundance, and to recollect their nomadic lifestyle while living a settled existence in towns or in the fields. In short, they must recollect a way of life that is not confirmed by any "framework" of their present reality. That is the exceptional situation of a counterfactual memory. It keeps present to the mind a yesterday that conflicts with every today. (Assmann 2006: 53)

In Assmann's view, the concerted effort to preserve counterfactual memory is otherwise alien to the ancient world; nothing like it exists, he maintains, in

Mesopotamia, Greece, or Egypt (Assmann 2006: 54). As the following sections will demonstrate, however, remembering privation in the midst of abundance was key to survival in the ancient Nile Valley. For this reason (among others), Egypt's inhabitants embedded memories of famine in literary works, in "prophetic" texts, and – most successfully – in ritual.

2 The Role of Witness Literature in Preserving Social Memory

The previous section devoted attention to accounts of catastrophic famines dating from Medieval and Ottoman times. While this choice may seem unusual in an Element devoted primarily to the experience of famine in pharaonic and Greco-Roman Egypt, it emphasizes two points. First, severe famines in Egyptian history would have been intensely traumatic for people who lived through them. Second, although such famines rarely struck twice within living memory, they occurred numerous times during the three millennia that separate Narmer from Constantine. After all, neither the population estimates for Egypt's Nile Valley nor the country's hydrology changed dramatically prior to the advent of the twentieth century. If anything, new technology, such as the *saqiya* water wheel, provided later Egyptians with an advantage over their pharaonic predecessors. This emphasis on the potential severity of famines and on the fact that terrible famines might strike at least once every century is vital, because recent scholarship tends to discount the personal attestations and creative reimaginings of the experience of famine in Egypt as either tendentious hyperbole or the pharaonic literary equivalent of a fashionable taste for *Sturm und Drang* (cf. Contardi 2015: 14–18; Gee 2015: 61–2; Moreno García 2015: 83; Schneider 2017: 312–14).[2]

In this section, I argue that the literature penned in response to the First Intermediate Period preserved memories of the effects of famine on Egyptian society, even if these memories were transmitted intergenerationally or were pertinent to troubles experienced later in Egypt's history. I also argue – drawing on diaries and memoirs penned by the survivors of near starvation – that the most "pessimistic" variants likely provide a more honest account of how it felt to live through such a time than the many autobiographical inscriptions that allude to famine. The authors of autobiographical texts have been plausibly charged with having exaggerated suffering to enhance their own accomplishments (Moreno García 1997). I argue the opposite, that in order to present themselves as patrons rather than profiteers elites glossed over the terrors and moral complexities of true famines.

Hero narratives that emerged from situations of near starvation during World War II tended to simplify and sanitize the ethically ambiguous aspects of their

---

[2] Important exceptions to this rule include Hassan 2007 and Gnirs 2015.

experience. Primo Levi famously observed that while the altruistic prisoners he knew at Auschwitz died quickly on the camp's starvation rations, the behavior of survivors necessarily fell into a "gray zone" (Levi 1988: 36–69). Certainly, the hundreds of diaries kept by those who slowly starved during World War II and the famine songs composed in Ethiopia and China bear a strong resemblance to the sentiments expressed by the narrators of Egyptian pessimistic literature.

Most of the ancient literature discussed in this section was either set in the long First Intermediate Period (c. 2160–1895) – stretching from the latter part of the Sixth Dynasty to the famines referenced by Heqanakht and others in the reign of Senwosret I – or influenced by its reception. It is therefore crucial to preface a discussion of these texts with a brief review of recent scientific studies that utilize a wide variety of methodologies. These studies conclude that the ecological situation prevailing with intermittent intensity during this period would have occasioned subsistence crises never previously experienced in the history of the pharaonic state. The point is not to argue that each famine in the pessimistic literature had a First Intermediate Period famine as its referent nor to deny that beneficent floods and relative normalcy also occurred during this long stretch of time. It is, rather, to emphasize that, like the waves of famines and Black Death that beset Europe in the fourteenth century, the famines of the long First Intermediate Period set the benchmark for subsequent suffering.

2.1 Scientific Studies Lend Credence to Ancient Reports of Suffering

Recent scientific studies are beginning to shift Egyptological thinking regarding the role of climate change in hastening the end of the Old Kingdom and exacerbating political fragmentation and strife during the subsequent First Intermediate Period (Creasman 2020). The ecological shift that brought severe drought and radically reduced Nile flooding has been dubbed the 4.2 kiloyear BP aridification event. While more work is needed to clarify the character of climate change at this time, the following studies provide a sampling of how a multiplicity of techniques in a variety of places have yielded similar results. At Lake Tana, the source of the Blue Nile in Ethiopia, magnetic and geochemical coring revealed "a period of intense dryness" at roughly 2200 BCE, during the reign of Pepi II (c. 2216–2153), the last monarch of the Old Kingdom. The dry spell coincided with "a short period when outflow ceased from Lake Victoria, at the source of the White Nile," suggesting that reduced Nile flow contributed to the collapse of the Old Kingdom state (Marshall et al. 2011: 147, 159). Even Karl Butzer, who had argued forcefully in the past against climate-driven explanations for the collapse of the Old Kingdom, asserted in 2012 that the limnological record of Lake Turkana in Ethiopia indicated that minimal influx from the Blue Nile "probably unleashed a severe subsistence crisis that helped trigger an economic breakdown near the end of Pepi II's reign" (Butzer 1997: 245, 261; 2012: 3633–4).

With reference to suffering to the north and east of Egypt, tree-ring sequences from cedar samples indicate an offset from 2200–1900 BCE consistent with the climate change postulated by the 4.2 kyr BP event (Manning et al. 2014: 401, 414). A team of scientists examining brine sediments in the northern Red Sea reached a similar conclusion. The timing and strength of the reconstructed environmental changes around 4.2 kyr BP, they stated, are suggestive of "a major drought event" that affected northern Africa as well as Mesopotamia (Arz, Lamy, and Pätzold 2006: 432, 440). Such a severe drought would have placed stress on neighboring populations and thus almost certainly have resulted in the large-scale movement of climate refugees toward Egypt's Nile Delta, as will be discussed later (Höflmayer 2015: 123).

Within Egypt, effects of region-wide droughts and reduced Nile flows have been identified in numerous sediment samples. Cores taken from Burullus Lagoon in the Nile Delta, for example, show decreases c. 4.2 cal kyr BP in Cyperaceae pollen and increases in microscopic charcoal, which are characteristic of low Nile flows and "extreme regional and global aridity events." Comparable levels of these trace elements had not occurred for 800 years and would not again appear for 1,200 years (Bernhardt, Horton, and Stanley 2012: 615, 617). So too, recent coring at Saqqara revealed a meter-thick layer of dune sands over areas upon which crops had previously grown (Hassan et al. 2017: 62). Such a situation could easily have been observed by Ipuwer, the purported author of a text discussed in this section, when he complained that "the desert is throughout the land" (Enmarch 2008: 223). At Saqqara as well as Abusir, Giza, and Abu Roash, other geomorphological studies indicated that the deposition of slope and aeolian deposits occurred at the same time as dramatically low floods. These low floods, in combination with unusually intense bursts of rain, triggered catastrophic flash floods that left ample evidence of their destruction in the Memphite cemeteries and appear to have led to significant innovations in tomb design (Welc and Marks 2014: 131; Kuraszkiewicz 2016).

The catastrophic co-occurrence of low floods and intense rain may also account for the fact that Lake Qarun was effectively cut off from the Nile and received, via flash floods, a significant input of sand. As a result, the lake would have shrunk significantly (Marks et al. 2017: 76). Cores from Lake Qarun also indicated "the quick shift of the ITCZ southward occurring at ca. 4200–4000 cal. yrs BP," which resulted in hyper-aridification (Zhao et al. 2017: 27). Yet another project that examined cores from Lake Qarun and soil sediments in the Saqqara-Memphis region concluded that c. 4.2 kyr BP the Nile Valley saw "reduced Nile flood discharge, invasion of the Nile Valley by dune sand, and possible degradation of the Delta floodplain as revealed by proxy sedimentological data" (Hamdan et al. 2016: 97). This trifecta of low floods, widespread aridity, and occasional but unusually heavy downpours, Fabian Welc and Leszek Marks conclude, "caused a rapid collapse of the Old Kingdom at about 4200 cal BP" (Welc and Marks 2014: 124).

Ancient records suggest that disruptive inundations occurred periodically over the course of the eight hundred years or so that the Egyptian state had been unified. Never before, however, does there appear to have been such a dramatic and extended ecological downturn. Erratic Nile floods repeated in close succession had the power to cripple or unseat a central government and to significantly hamper attempts at recovery. As discussed in the previous section, starvation, the vulnerability of malnourished bodies to disease, and political unrest often resulted in mass mortality. Thus, even when beneficent floods resumed, labor shortages prevented the repair of crucial agricultural infrastructure (Borsch 2005: 34–52). Despite their various silences, exaggerations, and idiosyncrasies, the literary sources discussed in the next section provide an ancient commentary on the experience of individuals forced to live through such turbulent times.

2.2 The Reception of the First Intermediate Period in Literature

Communal tragedy has the potential to fundamentally transform society. More recent examples include the Black Death, the Great Famine that caused over a million deaths between 1845 and 1852 in Ireland, and the two World Wars, each of which created seismic shifts in the world and worldview of their survivors. In pharaonic Egypt, the body of literature that was written in reaction to the First Intermediate Period is unprecedented in its exploration of personal trauma, societal turmoil, and the fallibility of rulers. Before focusing on the texts that I argue fit the classification of "witness literature" – namely literature written during or in response to a traumatic event with the goal of conveying how it felt, or must have felt, to live through it – it is useful to begin with a survey of the narratives that directly address the long First Intermediate Period.[3]

---

[3] The philological studies and secondary literature on each of the texts referred to in this Element are voluminous and encompass debates that, regrettably, cannot be surveyed here.

2.2.1 Tale of the Eloquent Peasant

This story is set in the reign of the Herakleopolitan king Nebkaure Khety, who exercised control over the north of Egypt in the Ninth or Tenth Dynasty (c. 2118–1980). Because the protagonist's family has to subsist on a dwindling supply of the previous year's barley (an especially drought-resistant grain), he travels from the Wadi Natrun to the Nile Valley to sell his wares and obtain provisions. As a character in the story remarks, a peasant would only make such a journey if there were nothing in his house (Simpson 2003: 30). After one of the peasant's donkeys takes a bite of barley from the field of an avaricious estate manager who forced a detour through his field as a snare, his goods are confiscated. While pleading his case to the authorities, the peasant critiques a society in which nobles perpetrate crimes, towns are unsafe, judges and tax collectors steal, and the elite – instead of sharing resources and allowing the poor to buy on credit – hoard grain and devour it selfishly (Simpson 2003: 31, 35, 39). After presenting his case repeatedly and being beaten in the process, the peasant receives restitution and compensation.

Scholars differ as to whether the text, which survives in four copies, was composed in the first half of the Twelfth Dynasty (Parkinson 2002: 50, 297; Allen 2015: 229) or the second (Stauder 2013: 509). The latter date takes the composition far enough from the First Intermediate Period that the peasant's reproaches may well be directed at contemporary wrongs (Simpson 1991: 97–9). It is notable, however, that *Eloquent Peasant* was found together with – and written in the same hand as – the *Tale of Sinuhe*, which deals with tumultuous events set in the reign of Senwosret I. On another occasion the two texts shared the same papyrus (Allen 2015: 55, 229). The story's association with the *Tale of Sinuhe* as well as the deeply pessimistic *Dispute between a Man and His Ba*, discussed in the next section, suggests it was composed and curated by scribes interested in exploring themes relevant to the long First Intermediate Period.

2.2.2 Teaching for Merikare

King Khety, potentially the same Herakleopolitan king who followed the trial in *Eloquent Peasant* with interest, purportedly composed this text to pass on wisdom to his son and heir concerning statecraft. Violent mobs of the indigent and hungry, he advises, should be pacified with food from storehouses (Demidchik 2011: 69, n. 76).[4] Potential rebels and their followers, however, would better be killed or co-opted, while immigrants should be rounded up and

---

[4] According to an alternative reading, rabble rousers should be locked up in the workhouse (Simpson 2003: 155).

either expelled or settled in buffer zones and taxed (Simpson 2003: 153–4, 157, 160–1, 163). The king recommends peaceful relations with Upper Egyptian vassals and amnesty for their debts, asking "if someone has no grain, can he give it?" Finally, he expresses regret that his own soldiers had plundered cemeteries during former conflicts (Simpson 2003: 159, 163). If his son follows his advice, the old king assures him, "The Nile flood will cause you no worry by failing to come" (Simpson 2003: 160).

The text is known from three mid-to-late-Eighteenth-Dynasty papyri and a Ramesside ostracon. Suggestions for its date of composition range from the Tenth Dynasty, the Eleventh or early Twelfth Dynasty, the high Twelfth Dynasty, or the Eighteenth Dynasty (cf. Quack 1992: 120–36; Parkinson 2002: 50, 316; Gnirs 2000, Demidchik 2011). While the text may have been composed to garner sympathy for the "thankless and difficult nature of kingship" (Enmarch 2008: 62), the pervasive social unrest that the old king is confronted with resonates with evidence from the First Intermediate Period and from other eras during which the central government had faltered or failed in the aftermath of famine (Sections 1.1, 4.2; Morris 2022). Joachim Quack's suggestion that the text had already been quoted in a stele dating to the reign of Senwosret I is tentatively supported by Karl Jansen-Winkeln (2017: 123), who sees nothing to support a date later than the Twelfth Dynasty.

2.2.3 Prophecy of Neferti

In this tale of wonder, the rise of the first king of the Twelfth Dynasty (c. 1939) is predicted by a lector priest whom the Fourth-Dynasty king Snefru (c. 2543–2510) summons to amuse him with "a few fine words and elegant phrases" (Simpson 2003: 215). Much to the king's surprise, the priest instead launches into a terrifying description of the political and social chaos that he predicts will rack the country during the long First Intermediate Period. Neferti foresees a Nile flood so low that it could be forded on foot and the consequent failure of the harvest. The ensuing unrest, he claims, will cause the overthrow of nobles, insecurity due to in-migration by desert dwellers, a radical shift in the social hierarchy, internal warfare, division within families, and death on a scale that leads to the cessation of mourning or even empathy (Simpson 2003: 216–19).

Although the earliest known copy of this text dates to the first half of the Eighteenth Dynasty, its prediction of the coming of Amenemhat I as savior has led most Egyptologists to assign it to the reign of that king or one of his successors (cf. Parkinson 2002: 49, 304). According to Jan Assmann, its description of chaos presents "exactly the same picture of fear and anguish, violence and disarray, hardship and hunger that forms the backdrop for

Ankhtifi's self-representation" (Assmann 2003: 109). A recent study has refuted earlier attempts to see a Second Intermediate or Eighteenth Dynasty date, thereby obviating the necessity to explain the text as a backdated encomium to strong kingship (Gnirs 2006; Stauder 2013: 518; Jansen-Winkeln 2017: 121). While the harrowing portrait of civilization unraveled is strikingly similar to the emphatically pessimistic *Admonitions of Ipuwer*, *Neferti*'s happy ending may have rendered it palatable to scribal teachers, who often integrated it into their curriculum (Enmarch 2008: 25).

2.2.4 Teaching of King Amenemhat I

The premise of this text is that the assassinated king Amenemhat I (c. 1939–1910; Figure 6), whose murder also set the popular *Tale of Sinuhe* into motion, returns to provide advice to his son, Senwosret I (c. 1920–1875). As in *Merikare*, the narrating pharaoh expresses vulnerability – admitting that he was attacked by those in his inner circle and adding with humility that "no one is strong at night, and none can fight by himself" (Simpson 2003: 169). About his reign, Amenemhat takes care to say "I was one who increased the grain, (for I was) favored by [*the grain god*] Nepri; [*the flood god*] Happy gave me honor on every field, so that none hungered during my years" (Simpson 2003: 169). Yet despite his success in reuniting the country, subduing foreigners, and building monuments, his populace remained riven by discord (Simpson 2003: 170).

First attested in the early Eighteenth Dynasty, the text is narrated as if spoken posthumously. In the Ramesside Period, it seems to have been attributed to a well-known scribe named Khety, who purportedly composed "the papyrus with *The Teaching of Sehotepibre* (= *Amenemhat*) when he (Amenemhat I) was

Figure 6 Lintel of Amenemhat I (Metropolitan Museum of Art 08.200.5), public domain https://commons.wikimedia.org/wiki/File: Lintel_of_Amenemhat_I_and_Deities_MET_DP322051.jpg

at rest (dead)" (P. Chester Beatty IV vso 6.13–14, trans. Parkinson 2002: 91). Scholars have tended to conclude that the text was composed on Senwosret I's orders to bolster his perceived legitimacy, to laud his father, and perhaps also to excuse his own seemingly excessive caution (Simpson 1996: 441; Parkinson 2002: 30–1, 49, 90–1, 316–17). Others suggest that Amenemhat advised his son after surviving his assassination attempt (Thériault 1993: 157–60) or view the story as an imaginative response to *Sinuhe* and date it anywhere from the late Twelfth to the Eighteenth Dynasty (Stauder 2013: 508, 518, 520, though see the recent refutation of a date later than the Twelfth Dynasty by Jansen-Winkeln 2017: 122). Both *Amenemhat* and *Sinuhe* became core texts in the New Kingdom scribal curriculum, along with the *Hymn to the Nile* with which *Amenemhat* shared a papyrus and a variety of associated contexts (Simpson 1996: 442; Hagen 2013: 86–8; 2019: 179). As will be discussed in Section 4, the hymn enumerates the dire consequences for Egypt should the Nile fail to rise.

The authors of the four works just discussed drew for inspiration upon the politically and socially fraught long First Intermediate Period. While the reigns of Amenemhat I and Senwosret I are not generally viewed as relevant to the First Intermediate Period, neither war nor famine ceased with the reunification of Egypt by the Eleventh-Dynasty king Mentuhotep II (c. 2009–1959). Barely twenty years after that king's death, Amenemhat I besieged Egyptian cities in his bid to exert control over the Nile Valley, and later he may have been assassinated in a palace coup. His son and co-regent's reign saw at least two famines. As discussed in Section 1, Heqanakht restricted his family's rations in year 7 as a low Nile depleted his resources to 25.5 sacks of barley and emmer – significantly diminished from the 185 or so sacks he stockpiled in good years (Allen 2002: 135). Concerning the second famine, which took place less than two decades later, an overseer of priests reported, "A low Nile came to pass during Regnal year 25, and I did not allow (my) nome to hunger. I gave it Upper Egyptian barley and emmer. I did not permit misery to take place – until high Niles came (again)" (Simpson 2001: 8). Whether this famine occurred over one low Nile or a series is unclear, since Amenemhat of Beni Hasan boasted of enduring longer hardships:

> There was no pauper in my surroundings, no hungry man in my time. There came years of hunger. Then I plowed all the fields of the Oryx nome to its southern and northern border, so that I fed its inhabitants, provided its supplies, and none hungered in it. … Then came high Niles, rich in barley and emmer, rich in all things, and I did not exact the arrears of the field. (Lichtheim 1988: 139)

Literate individuals who lived through the famines in the reign of Senwosret I had every right to expect similar disasters to strike again within their lifetime.

The milieu of these tales is broadly consonant with information about the severity of droughts and Nile flood failures gleaned from scientific studies, autobiographical inscriptions, parallels from later Egyptian famines, and other archaeological and textual sources of social history.[5] During droughts and famines the rapacious behavior of some elites exacerbated famine, leading to mob violence and rebellion. Law and order evidently broke down; attempts by regional rulers to impose order and restore trust in gods and governments were halting; and deaths due to famine, disease, and war led to empathy fatigue and declining societal investment in mourning and mortuary rituals.

2.3 Witness Literature

These four fictional works were most likely written at different times, in different genres, for different purposes. Apart from the *Prophecy of Neferti*, which receives greater attention in Section 3, they provide but a faint flavor of what it must have *felt* like to live through a period during which three of the four horsemen of the apocalypse – famine, war, and pestilence – ran roughshod. Three works yet to be discussed, however, *do* purport to provide first-hand narratives of intense suffering. The problem for modern Egyptologists in assessing these works is that no contemporary scholar has experienced either a series of low Niles or the effects of mass starvation on body, soul, and society. The historical account of Nilotic famines, explored in Section 1, aims to address the first deficit. For the second, diaries and witness literature authored by individuals who experienced starvation during World War II can serve as comparanda.

Elie Wiesel, who wrote a memoir of his childhood in a Nazi death camp, received the Nobel Peace Prize some forty years after the Holocaust for his role as a "messenger to mankind." His attempts to speak the unspeakable and thereby to combat what he felt to be an encroaching cultural amnesia constituted part of a wider postwar movement. In a lecture, he asserted, "If the Greeks invented tragedy, the Romans the epistle, and the Renaissance the sonnet, our generation invented a new literature, that of testimony" (quoted in Engdahl 2002: 5–6). Because the Nazis employed starvation as a tool of war in their blockade strategies and death camps, historians seeking to understand the psychological and sociological effect of such tactics find the correspondence, diaries, oral histories, and memoirs written in and about World War II indispensable.

Fictional narratives written by survivors or, more often, by others who attempt to channel their voices and thus speak for those whose sufferings rendered them mute have proved similarly important. In a review of Jerzy

---

[5] In addition to the texts cited elsewhere, see Vandier 1936; Morris 2022.

Kosinski's novel *The Painted Bird,* Wiesel observed that even as information about wartime atrocities continued to be revealed through historical research, its emotive power seemed to fade. "As always when a mystery is confronted, knowledge becomes a handicap," he wrote. "The more facts we accumulate, the less we understand their texture" (Wiesel 1965). Thus, he maintained, writers able to successfully communicate the experience of sufferers serve a vital social role.

The authors of the three texts discussed in this Element – *Dispute between a Man and His Ba, Lamentations of Khakheperreseneb,* and *Admonitions of Ipuwer* – may have aimed to preserve social memory by imbuing it with affect. None explicitly states the time in which their narrative is set, although the fact that the *Dispute* was found together with *Eloquent Peasant* and *Sinuhe* strongly suggests a referent in the long First Intermediate Period. Intertextual clues also provide links to this famously troubled time. The fact that the texts are not unambiguously anchored to a specific event, however, as well as the seemingly hyperbolic anguish expressed by their narrators, has led to their frequent dismissal as sources for social history. Yet both in form and content, these texts resonate with first-hand accounts of individuals suffering from starvation and with witness literature produced in the aftermath of World War II.

2.3.1 Dispute between a Man and His Ba

As a woman named Ankhet ("life") watches and tries to help, a sick man hovering at the cusp of death enters into a dialogue with an aspect of his soul – his ba (Escolano-Poveda 2017: 35; Figure 7). The two discuss whether he should embrace death, even though he would have to do so without having constructed a tomb. Surprisingly, his ba advises him not to worry about burial. The fate of those who built magnificent tombs, after all, is the same as those whose bodies lay exposed to the elements. Instead of fretting, the sick man should "follow a good time" and forget his care (Allen 2011: 171). Such advice, however, is easier given than taken. In his environs, lawlessness and theft are commonplace, even among neighbors. Relations between friends and family have been poisoned, and empathy is replaced by indifference (Allen 2011: 175–7). While there is no overt indication that the social turmoil results from famine, the man's complaints had all been foreseen by Neferti in a vision that began with a low Nile. Moreover, to illustrate the world's ills his ba relates the story of a husband who was furious with his wife for preventing him from eating when he was hungry (Allen 2011: 171–3). This parable would be wildly incongruous if the man's hunger had not been extremely severe, as it is paired with a tale about a man's family being torn apart by crocodiles.

Figure 7 A mummy and its ba, Theban tomb 277 (photograph by Daniel
Warne)

The only extant copy of *Dispute* dates to the late Middle Kingdom, although
it may have been composed as early as the reign of Senwosret II (Parkinson
2002: 50; Allen 2011: 9). Not surprisingly, it never enjoyed the popularity of
either *Eloquent Peasant* or *Sinuhe*, the two manuscripts with which it was
found. Darker in tone than either, it offered its reader neither intrepid heroes
nor hope for redemption. Interestingly, however, the text's skepticism toward
the utility of building tombs to prepare for an afterlife and its exhortation to live
for the moment may have been reimagined in a harper's song that appeared in an
Amarna Period tomb at Saqqara (Lichtheim 1945: 191–4; Allen 2011: 147–8).
If its attribution to a King Intef (necessarily of the First or Second Intermediate
Period) was pseudepigraphic, Akhenaten's high official likely felt that the last
comparable shock to Egypt's ideological system took place in the aftermath of
state collapse.

2.3.2 Lamentations of Khakheperreseneb

Like *Dispute*, this text represents an anguished appeal from an individual to
a component of his composite soul – in this instance, his heart (Figure 8). After
pondering how to devise new words to express unprecedented and seemingly
unspeakable grief, the narrator describes the chaos and misery that engulfs him.
"[O]ne year," he says, "is more troublesome than the next . . .. Mourning is

Figure 8 Wooden writing board and text of *Lamentations of Khakheperreseneb* (British Museum EA 5645) © The trustees of the British Museum

everywhere. Towns and districts are in lamentation . . . . Every day one wakes to suffering" (Simpson 2003: 212–13). Unrest and exploitation are pervasive, offerings to the gods occur no more, social order is disrupted, and wrongs are perpetrated by *all* people, even those not normally given to such behavior (Simpson 2003: 212–13). The man's heart, when it answers back, can only commiserate (Hagen 2019: 200).

Because Khakheperreseneb's name incorporated the prenomen of Senwosret II (c. 1845–1837), he could not have lived during the long First Intermediate Period (c. 2160–1895 BCE). Presuming he was born in Senwosret II's reign, however, he is likely to have experienced the erratic floods in the reign of Amenemhat III (c. 1818–1773; Bell 1975: 256–9; Creasman 2020: 27–8) that may have destabilized the dynasty and/or to have heard tales from survivors of the famines that took place in the reign of Senwosret I (c. 1920–1875).[6] The narrator's evident desire to find new words to express the unutterable pain of living is ironic, since his composition echoes the conceit of the *Dispute* so closely. Likewise, some suggest that certain turns of phrase, his address to his heart, and his role as a Heliopolitan priest may have been inspired by *Neferti* (Parkinson 2002: 200, 203, Assmann 2003: 171). Although Khakheperreseneb was memorialized as a revered sage in the Ramesside Period, alongside Neferti (as well as Ipuwer and

---

[6] A recent redating to the early Thirteenth Dynasty or later in the Second Intermediate Period has been convincingly refuted (Stauder 2013: 510; Jansen-Winkeln 2017: 119).

the writer of the *Teaching of Amenemhat*), the text enjoyed far less success in the scribal curriculum. A recent identification of *Khakheperreseneb* on two Second Intermediate Period writing boards from Thebes has doubled its known attestations (Parkinson 2002: 30–32; Hagen 2019: 206–7).

2.3.3 Admonitions of Ipuwer

Of these texts, the *Admonitions of Ipuwer* (Figure 9) contains by far the most comprehensive and specific catalog of social woes. According to the narrator, a drought pervades the land, withering even barley. People steal food from one another and resort to consuming anything remotely edible. Even the rich are hungry, offering their valuables as well as their children for sale. Theft and banditry are rampant and nothing is sacred: tombs and temples are targeted, as people desperately search for goods to sell for bread. Luxury imports cease, while foreign peoples migrate into Egypt and compete for sustenance. Egyptians, too, migrate in search of food. Laborers who used to receive their salary in victuals go on strike due to lack of payment, and farmers refuse to pay taxes on crops they are unable to harvest. Out of desperation and anger, mobs storm government storehouses, destroy administrative and judicial records, and set prisoners free. Local governments, magnates, and even the king are

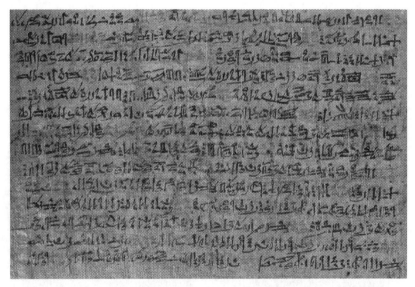

Figure 9 Section of Papyrus Leiden I 344 recto, *Admonitions of Ipuwer* (Rijksmuseum van Oudheden AMS 27 vel 4), public domain https://en .wikipedia.org/wiki/Ipuwer_Papyrus#/media/File:Papyrus_van_Ipoewer_- _Google_Art_Project.jpg

overthrown, and social hierarchies are not only disrupted but often inverted. Weakened immune systems and hunger lead to a near cessation of births, to infanticide, and to a mass mortality so overwhelming that burial rites are forsaken. Even among family members, no one has the emotional reserves to extend sympathy. People wish they had never been born, and many take their own lives (Enmarch 2008: 221–40).

Outraged, Ipuwer confronts the Lord of All with a "reproach to god" (or perhaps the king) – a genre that may have been an innovation of the Eleventh Dynasty (Morenz 2010: 265–7). Yet despite his emotional appeal, no hope for salvation is offered. Indeed, one of the most optimistic statements in the text is that the children of the pious man will "witness the overflowing of the flood" (Enmarch 2008: 234). In this manner, *Ipuwer* differs from the far more popular *Neferti*. While Ipuwer was remembered as an "overseer of singers" and honored alongside Khakheperreseneb and other famous authors, only a single manuscript (dating to the Nineteenth Dynasty) survives. Suggestions as to its date of composition range from the late Old Kingdom to the New Kingdom, and much depends on whether intertextual similarities indicate a familiarity with *Dispute*, *Neferti*, and the *Teaching of Amenemhat* or vice versa. Most recent studies favor a date in the early Thirteenth Dynasty – a time of incipient upheaval (Enmarch 2008: 24–6; Stauder 2013: 509). *Ipuwer* is variously regarded as a reflection of a historical reality, a theodicy, or a festival text that denigrates chaos in its promotion of order (Enmarch 2008: 4–8).

Although the description of chaos in *Ipuwer* is often dismissed as poetic exaggeration, it conforms to the trajectory of a "typical" famine. As Cormac Ó Gráda explains,

> No two famines are the same, yet, superficially at least, most have a lot in common. The usual symptoms might include high food prices beyond the reach of the poor; increases in evictions, and in crime and antisocial behavior; vagrancy and migration in search of employment and charity; rising unemployment; hunger-induced reductions in the birth and marriage rates; protests and resistance that give way to apathy and hopelessness as the crisis worsens; early philanthropic efforts that, in the more protracted crises, give way to donor fatigue; fear of, and lack of compassion toward, the victims; and, above all, increases in mortality from disease and starvation. (Ó Gráda 2015: 1)

With respect to Egypt, scientific studies, attestations by individuals who lived during times of famine, archaeological evidence, and chronicles of particularly severe Medieval and Ottoman Nilotic famines lend credence to much of *Ipuwer*'s description of life in the midst of famine. Rather than recapitulate arguments mounted elsewhere (Sections 1.1, 2.1, 4.2; Morris 2006, 2020,

2022; Hassan 2007), this section places *Dispute, Khakheperreseneb,* and *Ipuwer* in dialogue with works written by people actively starving, by survivors of starvation, and by "belated witnesses," as Michael Levine (2006) terms authors who reimagine historical trauma as an act of empathy. By virtue of this dialogue between ancient and modern accounts, it is clear that the pessimism of these three works is in fact truer in tone to the lived experience of famine than the "vigour, self-confidence, and pride in achievement" that typify First Intermediate Period autobiographical narratives (Seidlmayer 2000: 146).

The psychic wounds of survivors of trauma, as Levine and others have noted, impact the lives of their children. While a reduced capacity for nurturing may bear ill effects, recent studies have demonstrated that the situational depression of a famine victim can be passed on in utero to her child, manifesting in an elevated susceptibility to depression (Stein et al. 2009: 909, 913; Li et al. 2018: 579, 583–4). Some adult children remain indifferent to or resentful of the tragedy that haunted their parents, but others process and communicate this pain through imaginative witnessing, as is attested by the many historically informed novels and poems produced by children of Holocaust survivors (Levine 2006; McGlothlin 2006). Although some critics express deep discomfort when anyone who has not directly experienced trauma channels it, others maintain that "Literature is supplementary, not antithetical, to history: it allows, and in the best instances demands readers to universalize, empathize, to visualize and imagine, not merely to be informed" (Kaiser 2010). Like first-hand accounts, such works have the potential to serve as "messengers to mankind."

Historical chronicles of Medieval and Ottoman famines in Egypt describe in vivid detail the same dynamics described in pessimistic literature, but their authors rarely attempt to convey how *felt* to live in a time of famine, social chaos, and mass mortality. Because the victims of famine have historically remained mute, the individuals who corresponded or kept diaries while they slowly starved in besieged cities, ghettos, or death camps in World War II constitute an important exception. The remainder of this section places their writings in conversation with the most pessimistic of Egypt's authors. Writers who lived in Leningrad prove particularly informative, as German soldiers remained outside the city for the entire 872-day siege and desisted from shelling it for long periods of time. For the *blokadniki,* as those trapped in the city referred to themselves, the most fearsome enemy was hunger. Eight hundred thousand or so civilians died in the siege, the vast majority of starvation (Peri 2017: 4). Five important lessons for historians interested in famine can be abstracted from this cross-cultural and cross-temporal comparison.

2.4 Overarching Lessons Concerning Starvation

2.4.1 When Starving People Are Forced to Share Food, Love Often Turns to Hate

A source of anguish in pessimistic literature is the irrevocable ruptures that occurred among family members. Ipuwer laments that sustenance was often stolen, even within households, and that toddlers – before they could speak – learned to defend their food (Enmarch 2008: 239). In this unbearable world, brothers not only ceased protecting one another but came to blows (Enmarch 2008: 227, 232, 238). The narrator of *Dispute* also bemoans a world in which brothers stole from one another and became enemies (Allen 2011: 175). So too, as previously mentioned, his ba tells of a man who reacted with fury when his wife asked him not to eat until the designated time: "When he turns back to his house, he is like another man, his wife pleading to him. He doesn't listen to her, offended and unreceptive to those of the household" (Allen 2011: 173). Similar stories abound in the diaries of the *blokadniki*.

As the siege of Leningrad progressed, writers increasingly remarked on the dissolution of social ties. During the winter of 1941–1942, when rations – if shared equitably – were not sufficient to sustain life, rates of abandonment and theft within families skyrocketed. Indeed, in her study of these diaries, Alexis Peri notes that practically the only familial relationships that remained loving were carried on by mail (Peri 2017: 89–125). Otherwise, the stress of constant hunger led to deep-seated resentment at having to share food and to the suspicion (often well founded) that others in the household were pilfering. Sibling rivalries, present in times of plenty, now developed murderous overtones (Peri 2017: 98–9), and bonds between parents and children and between husbands and wives also turned antagonistic. The devolution of Elena Kochina's happy marriage is documented in her diary. As her husband began to steal food that he should have shared with her and their infant daughter, Kochina came to neither trust nor love him. The couple increasingly withdrew into their own silent suffering (Kochina 2014: 43, 45–6, 52, 71–2, 94).

The observations of Lydia Ginzburg help place Kochina's reaction in perspective. "People will say: the ties of love and blood make sacrifice easier," she writes. "No, it's much more complicated than that. So painful, so fearful was it to touch one another, that in propinquity, at close quarters, it was hard to distinguish love from hatred – towards those one couldn't leave" (Ginzburg 2016: 7). Another diarist, Arkadii Lepkovich, whose own loving marriage similarly turned to ashes, noted how typical this was: "A mother wishes death for her child, and a husband for his wife, and vice versa . . . . The whole city has become this way because the battle for life has brought despair to every living individual" (Peri 2017: 102). A couplet from an Ethiopian famine song expresses much the same sentiment from the perspective of a child: "Ah, Year Seventy-Seven, I wish I was not born! My own mother snatching away, the scraps of food in my hand" (Azeze 1998: 59–60).

2.4.2 Empathy toward Others Ceases as Starvation and Mass Mortality Deaden Emotions

Among the most tragic observations made by the writers of pessimistic literature is that in the midst of misery fellow sufferers offer neither solace nor empathy. According to Ipuwer, officials shunned those who cried out (Enmarch 2008: 222). The narrator of *Dispute* felt the issue to be even more widespread, noting that loving relations between family and friends had dissolved and that "kindness has perished" (Allen 2011: 175–7). In his prediction, Neferti foresaw the same:

> None will lie awake fasting at the time of death, for each man's heart cares for himself alone. None will make mourning today, for hearts have completely turned from it. A man will sit and turn his back, while one murders another. ... Every mouth is full of 'Take pity on me.' ... One answers a (man's) remark by a hand which lashes out with a stick. Instead of speaking, one kills him, for speech strikes the heart like fire, and none can endure what issues forth from the mouth. (Simpson 2003: 218)

Blokadniki often reported with alarm that the suffering of others had ceased to affect them and that any complaints appeared grossly self-indulgent. "People were all in the same situation," Lydia Ginzburg writes. "All were monstrously unrestrained and out of control. On the street you couldn't ask someone the time or how to get anywhere. In answer you would receive only abuse" (Ginzburg 2016: 163). Even corpses – stacked like "woodpiles" outside buildings or rotting in inhabited apartments because survivors lacked the strength to move them – had lost their power to shock or sadden (Pleysier 2008: 102, 104; Kochina 2014: 62, 86; Figure 10). In the grip of starvation, embitterment and indifference came to replace sorrow (Ginzburg 2016: 54–5; Pleysier 2008: 147). Ginzburg's lightly fictionalized alter ego, Otter ("autre" or "auteur") – upon whom she displaced her guilt for inflicting verbal abuse on her starving mother – analyzed the phenomenon this way: "Millions of deaths (the quantitative factor) are terrible only if the death of one person is terrible. If that *one* has no special importance then neither have the millions" (Ginzburg 2016: 147). Nonetheless, witnesses to such hellish scenes knew that their indifference was deeply wrong.

Figure 10 Bodies delivered to the Volkovo cemetery in Leningrad, October 1, 1942, Creative Commons (photograph by Boris Kudoyarov) https://commons .wikimedia.org/wiki/File:RIAN_archive_216_The_Volkovo_cemetery.jpg

Such a realization led Sofia Ostrovskaia, who recalled watching her mother's death throes with little emotion, to demand of her diary "Where is my heart?" (Peri 2017: 63).

2.4.3 As Anguish Turns Inward, the Fragmented "I" Becomes the Sole Empathetic Confidant

One of the attractions of death for the narrator of *Dispute* was that, as he put it, "I am loaded with need for lack of an intimate. To whom can I speak today?" (Allen 2011: 177). While Ipuwer directs his rage outward toward the Lord of All, the narrator of *Dispute* and Khakheperreseneb turn inward and confess their anguish to aspects of their own souls. Both the ba (addressed in *Dispute*) and the heart (addressed by Khakheperreseneb) were components of the composite self in both life and death. The author of *Dispute* envisions his ba as an active interlocutor in his struggle over whether to surrender to death or to fight for life, while Khakheperreseneb's heart acts as his confessor and emotional lifeline. "O would that I had a heart that knew how to suffer," he writes. "I would load it with phrases of misery, and I might drive off to it my suffering." He then addresses his heart, hoping for answers and solace (Simpson 2003: 213).

For Fela Szeps, a prisoner from the Grünberg camp in Poland, reconnecting with her heart through diary writing kept her sane in a world she no longer understood. Her heart, she wrote, "seeks some handhold to express indefinable pain, and perhaps the pencil will afford it such a handhold" (Goldberg 2017: 15). Amid starvation, Ginzburg experienced Cartesian dualism strongly, with her body "an emaciated envelope in the category belonging to the hostile world, and a soul located separately, somewhere inside the ribcage" (Ginzburg 2016: 8). For many individuals experiencing radical emotional isolation, diaries offer what Michael Levine terms "an addressable you" – the only truly safe interlocutor that remains (Levine 2006: 3, 7–8). Diary writing in situations of trauma often serves to cleave the self in two, leaving one entity that suffers and another that retains enough humanity to regard its counterpart with concern (Goldberg 2017: 34–6, 43, 250–1; Peri 2017: 64, 67–8, 71–2).

2.4.4 The Specter of Death May Be Welcome

Although Ipuwer's account of the dystopian world he inhabited is more descriptive than emotive, he notes that many committed suicide and others longed to die (Enmarch 2008: 223, 225). The narrator of *Dispute* certainly did. All that gave him pause was the knowledge that he would have neither a tomb nor a mortuary cult, a common predicament in times of widespread death and social upheaval. Although this text has long been interpreted as an internal debate about the advisability of suicide, the recent discovery of its introduction demonstrates that the narrator was in fact extremely ill. Therefore, he faced a decision of whether to fight for his life or surrender to oblivion (Escolano-Poveda 2017: 34–7).

The resemblance of the narrator's condition to the "dystrophic" state of advanced starvation, in which the bedridden sufferer typically loses the will to live, may not be coincidental. Kochina observed her husband fall into this state, noting with concern: "He doesn't believe in anything anymore – not in evacuation, not in victory, not in life" (Kochina 2014: 90). Such a person rarely had long to live. Ginzburg was an exception, and her account offers a first-hand description of a state similar, perhaps, to that experienced by the narrator of *Dispute*. In an essay titled "Paralysis (Confessions of a Survivor of Dystrophy)," she describes the willingness with which she and others embraced "a weakened immobility, a detachment from a fearful world .... Through immobility I gradually achieved the disappearance of the body. The loathsome, hostile, suffering body gave no further sign of its presence." The sensation of breathing and of the heartbeat were all that remained. "So I was rocked on the waves of illness. And without thinking about it, I knew that this was the way people went into the easy death of dystrophy. . . . But life was already beginning to shine through, with its surviving desires – the desire to live and the readiness to risk death – glimmering through the torpor" (Ginzburg 2016: 104–5).

This turn toward life, however, did not resolve in joy. Ginzburg writes that despite having survived and reentered the living world, she "agonizingly didn't want any physical contact with it. Everything was a painful irritation of the skin or mind" (Ginzburg 2016: 101). Even when rations improved in the spring of 1942 and in 1943, the *blokadniki* continued to suffer both physical and spiritual torment. As Vera Kostrovitskaia put it, "we *distrofiki*" still longed for death in August 1943. "Every morning," she wrote, "you open your eyes and again and again you realize with horror that you are still alive" (Peri 2017: 243).

2.4.5 Efforts to Express the Inexpressible Often Lead to Excesses That Are Received with Suspicion

Skeptics who view Egypt's pessimistic literature as ahistorical exercises in theodicy correctly note that, in the absence of historical specifics, the texts appear almost feverishly hyperbolic (Enmarch 2008: 39). The narrators' worlds are suffused with horror, anguish, and suffering. Khakheperreseneb, because he must have been born after the First Intermediate Period, is often charged with a particularly self-indulgent literary disingenuousness. In his introduction, for example, he states that he wishes he had recourse to "unknown speeches, erudite phrases in new language which has not yet been used, free from (the usual) repetitions, not the phrases of past speech which (our) forefathers spoke." With these expressions he would address his heart "that I might enlighten my grief to it, and that I might thrust onto it the weight which is on my back, (and speak) thoughts about what afflicts me, that I might express to it what I suffer through it, that I might speak, Yea, about my feelings!" (Simpson 2003: 212).

Out of a desire to spare themselves and others deeply disturbing memories – and to disassociate themselves from the perceived stigma of starvation – many survivors of the Leningrad blockade remained silent about their experiences. Yet some who attempted to talk were met with disbelief by younger people, who drew upon their own memories of "hunger" to argue that the hunger of the *blokadniki* was likely exaggerated (Adamovich and Granin 1983: 25–6; Kochina 2014: 27). As Primo Levi wrote, reflecting on his own experience at Auschwitz, however, the hunger faced in near starvation does not truly belong to the same semantic category as hunger experienced in ordinary life. A new language would have to be invented to convey its extremity (Levi 2015: 151–2). As Amos Goldberg, who studied the diaries of Holocaust survivors, put it, "When the shock is so great, not only is it impossible to find the appropriate words with which to represent it but language as a whole is paralyzed and the power of speech completely lost" (Goldberg 2017: 77). "Ultimately," he writes, "the hyperbolic expression conveys recognition of the fact that 'we have lost the ability to use words'" (Goldberg 2017: 38). Similarly characterized by anguish, bewilderment, and terror, deeply disturbing first-hand narratives of famine survivors often meet with skepticism (Arnold 1988: 17–19). The dilemma of how to speak the unspeakable appears timeless (Engdahl 2002: 10–11; Levine 2006: 11).

2.5 The Deliberate Avoidance of a Hero Narrative in the Most Pessimistic Literature Adds Authenticity

One feature that distinguishes the emphatically pessimistic texts from the First Intermediate Period autobiographies and even from *Neferti* is their refusal to identify heroes or provide redemptive framing. These authorial decisions not to sanitize or valorize lend the texts credibility as sources for the social history of famine in Egypt. Primo Levi argued in *The Drowned and the Saved* that hardships brought out the worst in people far more often than the good (Levi 1988: 49–50, 82). Elena Kochina felt much the same. In her diary, she wrote:

> Before the war many people, showing off, would adorn themselves with bravery, fidelity to principles, honesty – whatever they liked. The hurricane of war has torn off these rags. Now everyone has become what he was in fact, and not what he wanted to seem. Many have turned out to be pitiful cowards and scoundrels. (Kochina 2014: 42)

Even Kochina and Lydia Ginzburg, who sacrificed their own well-being for family members, did so grudgingly and often helped themselves before they helped others. As Ginzburg's alter ego expressed it, "I survived – that means I didn't sacrifice enough" (Ginzburg 2016: 7). The distinction between the recovering and the dying, another survivor stated, was between "the cruel" and "the weak" (Peri 2017: 187).

In the diaries penned during the siege, individuals who looked well while others suffered came under strong suspicion, so much so that when Kochina's husband managed to steal enough food to keep them from starving, he made sure not to shave or wash lest the neighbors catch on (Kochina 2014: 80–1; Peri 2017: 145–6). The healthy or wealthy had almost certainly stolen, profiteered, or otherwise engaged in illegal acts. Indeed, in the severest food crises, hero narratives that fall outside Primo Levi's "gray zone" are rare. As Kochina put it, "Heroism, self-sacrifice, the heroic feat – only those who are full or who haven't been hungry long are capable of these. As for us, we came to know a hunger that degraded and crushed us, that turned us into animals. May those who come after us and happen to read these lines have mercy upon us!" (Kochina 2014: 82).

Figure 11 Ankhtifi of Mo'Alla, a "hero" of the First Intermediate Period
(photograph by Stephen Harvey)

While the triumphalist First Intermediate Period narratives of individuals
who "buried the dead and nourished the living" bear little resemblance to first-
hand accounts of starvation, they do resemble many narratives penned afterward (Figure 11). Memories of trauma are famously malleable. Thus, some
details are mercifully forgotten, while others are edited to fit new narratives
(Levi 2015: 2436–47). Alexis Peri noted, for example, that in interviews former
blokadniki tended to showcase themes – like hard work, social solidarity, faith
in victory, and gratitude for the sacrifices of others – that were all but absent
from the words they wrote during the siege (Peri 2017: 8, 93). One diarist,
Georgii Kniazev, had predicted this state of affairs. "[W]hat will be written later,
in the form of memoirs," he wrote, "will be a far cry from what we are living
through now" (Peri 2017: 2).

2.6 The Problem with Encoding Memories of Extreme Suffering in Personal Narratives and Literature is Reception

The lack of heroes in first-hand accounts of starvation renders these narratives
deeply uncomfortable. During oral histories of the Leningrad blockade, survivors confessed that people who had never suffered found accounts of victim-
ization and aporia frustrating, uninteresting, depressing, or even improbable
(Adamovich and Granin 1983: 25–8). It is little wonder, then, that if stories got
told at all, they featured themes that their audiences were likely to understand

and admire. As Lydia Ginzburg put it, "the well-fed do not understand the hungry" (Ginzburg 2016: 77). Nor, it seems, do they particularly desire to.

Because personal testimony contradicted the "blockade myth," the Soviet government sought to suppress the diaries that it had originally encouraged its citizens to write (Peri 2017: 241–2, 246–9). Families, instead of being "a bastion of loyalty and sacrifice," for example, proved to be "a site of anguish" (Peri 2017: 91). Even when the prohibitions against accessing and publishing this material ended in the 1980s, the issue of reception remained. Elena Kochina, when preparing her diary for publication, prefaced it with this statement: "If I have managed to portray even to a small degree what the war brought with it – the despair, the fear, the hunger, the deprivations, the isolation, and the moral decline caused by unbearable suffering – then I will consider that I have done my part" (Kochina 2014: 28). The bleakness of this statement, and of her diary, stands in strong contrast to the publisher's back-cover blurb, which touts it as "a tribute to generosity and courage." So too, on the back of the anthology of Lydia Ginzburg's writings that appeared in 2016, the publisher stated that "Ginzburg created a paean to the dignity, vitality and resilience of the human spirit" – a sentiment with which virtually no one who could make their way through "A Story of Pity and Cruelty" would agree! The optimistic spin publishers added to starvation narratives or that guided the self-imposed edits of other writers (Peri 2017: 247) may be reminiscent of the scribal decision to embed a description of famine and attendant social unrest in a tale of wonder and thus to provide it with a happy ending. Certainly, these edits significantly enhanced *Neferti*'s readership in comparison to the three texts just discussed, while still conveying a sense of the terror, disorientation, and suffering that Egyptians experienced when droughts and low Niles coincided.

3 The Role of "Prophecy" in Preserving Social Memory

Common sense suggests that the most effective way to pass on the memory of a truly terrible famine to later generations would be to provide a personal testimony or to serve as a "belated witness" and embed tales of suffering in historical fiction. As argued in Section 2, however, the problem, then and now, has been in finding an audience willing to read these works and to lend them credence. It is thus significant that the only exception to the rule that the most pessimistic literature was little loved seems to have been the *Prophecy of Neferti*, which, anomalously, had been embedded into a fanciful tale and provided with a happy ending. Whether its evocation of the rise of Amenemhat I (c. 1939–1910) as savior was intended to legitimate that king's rule (or his dynasty's rule or, even, autocratic rule in general) or whether it was simply a device intended to entice scribal students to focus on the threat famines posed is unclear. What is fascinating, however, is that in the Greco-Roman period, famine narratives seem most frequently to have circulated in the context of prophecy.

This section discusses the roles that famine played in visions of the future as well as the purposes of these prophecies and the audiences they addressed. While it is highly unlikely that any of these works, save perhaps *Neferti*, aimed first and foremost to keep memories of famine fresh, the degree to which they succeeded is of interest. Rather than focusing on famine simply as a problem that required solving, Egyptian priests in the Greco-Roman period explored its efficacy as a punishing agent. Here, I argue that the long co-residency of a Jewish garrison community and priests of the god Khnum on the tiny island of Elephantine may have led to an interchange of ideas that ultimately influenced the character of Egyptian prophecy. Whether the weaponization of famine helped encode its effects in social memory remains a question, but it is fitting to begin with a review of the relevant texts.

3.1 Prophecy of Neferti

The introduction to the *Prophecy of Neferti* frames it as a tale of wonder in which a Heliopolitan lector priest of Bastet named Neferti is able to warn King Snefru (c. 2543–2510) about the chaos that would beset Egypt during the long First Intermediate Period (c. 2160–1895 BCE). The grimness of the world he conjures has its closest parallel in the *Admonitions of Ipuwer*. As addressed in Section 2, Neferti foresees a natural world gone awry: "The river of Egypt is empty, and the waters may be crossed on foot. Men search for water that the ships may sail, but the watercourse has become a river bank ... . The land perishes, for its fate has been ordained. Its produce has been laid waste and its harvest made desolate" (Simpson 2003: 216, 218). Even the sun has dimmed, due to Re having "withdrawn himself from men" (Simpson 2003: 218). Foreigners seeking sustenance immigrate to the Nile Valley, and crime surges. Nobles and institutions of government are overthrown; regional rulers raise taxes and fight one another; social ties fray, and the ubiquity of suffering and death saps both energy and enthusiasm for mourning (Simpson 2003: 216–20).

While the earliest manuscript of *Neferti* dates from the first half of the Eighteenth Dynasty, its "prediction" of the rise of the first ruler of the Twelfth Dynasty has led most Egyptologists to attribute it either to this king's reign or to one of his dynastic descendants (Section 2.2.3). The fact that the text achieved its greatest (known) popularity in the scribal curriculum of the Ramesside Period, however, suggests that its interest transcended partisan politics (Figure 12). Given the explicitly didactic purpose of compositions like P. Anastasi I, *Neferti* could well have offered

Figure 12 Ostracon with an excerpt of the *Prophecies of Neferti* (LACMA
M.80.203.196), public domain https://en.wikipedia.org/wiki/
Prophecy_of_Neferti#/media/File:Ostracon_with_Fragment_
from_the_Pessimistic_Literary_Piece_'The_Prophecies_of_Neferti'_
LACMA_M.80.203.196.jpg

a lesson to aspiring scribes in the disastrous consequences of famines for the social
and political world.

3.2 Famine Stele

Despite the evident popularity of *Neferti*, prophetic writing did not emerge as a genre
until the Ptolemaic Period. While not, strictly speaking, a prophecy, the *Famine Stele*
is close enough to merit discussion here. Carved upon a boulder at Sehel Island in the
First Cataract, near the temple of Khnum, the text is a cultic forgery presented as
a decree sent from the Third-Dynasty king Djoser (c. 2592–2566) to the Governor of
the domains of the South (Figure 13). It is set in the seventh year of a terrible famine
when the Nile had yet again failed to rise sufficiently:

> Grain was scarce, the kernels dried out, everything edible in short supply . . . .
> The child was in tears, the youth astray, and the elderly – their hearts were
> miserable, their legs drawn together, squatting on the ground with their arms
> held inward. The courtiers were in ruin, the temples sealed up, the chapels
> dusty, everything found wanting. (Simpson 2003: 387)

Desperate to help his people, the king consulted his lector priest Imhotep, a man
commemorated alongside Neferti and a few others in a New Kingdom papyrus
as "sages who foretold the future, that which came forth from their mouths took

Figure 13 The *Famine Stele*, on the island of Sehel, near Aswan, Egypt, Creative Commons (photograph by Morburre) Morburre: https://commons .wikimedia.org/wiki/User:Morburre

place" (Simpson 2003: 1). In his wisdom, Imhotep advised his king to seek counsel from Khnum, the god who controlled the flood. Having obtained Khnum's reassurance in a dream that he would once again grant beneficent floods, Djoser recorded his offering of thanks in a legal document that bestowed a great wealth of land, chattel, and property on the god's temple in perpetuity.

This purported legal document was, of course, the point of the inscription. Thus, it is likely that priests from the temple of Khnum had "discovered" the decree shortly after Ptolemy VI (180–145) had redirected the specified income from the Dodekaschoinos in northern Nubia to the nearby temple of Isis at Philae (Quack 2012: 346–8). Ptolemy VI's reign was indeed troubled by low Niles, which seem to have exacerbated internal conflicts. Like insufficient floods that occurred periodically from the reign of Ptolemy III to that of Cleopatra, these stemmed from volcanic activity that suppressed Ethiopia's annual monsoons (Manning 2018: 159–71). The stele not only asserted the rights of the temple of Khnum to income that had recently been diverted from it but also implicitly blamed current circumstances on a divine anger that any seer could have foretold. Khnum had once imposed misery on Egypt by virtue of a particularly severe famine, and now – the priesthood implicitly asserted – the god was doing it again.[7]

3.3 Prophecy of the Lamb

This text, written in Demotic, concerns a prophecy purportedly sent by the sun god Re and delivered through the medium of a lamb in the reign of the Twenty-fourth-Dynasty pharaoh Bakenrenef (c. 728–723). Although the sole surviving copy dates to the reign of Augustus (30 BCE–14 CE), a version was known to the early-third-century BCE priest Manetho, who wrote that in the reign of Bakenrenef "a lamb spoke" (Simpson 2003: 445). The lamb's prophecy is prefaced by an enigmatic statement that the "great water of Egypt will become .... " Presumably, the news was not good, for the lamb states that although farmers "will plow a quantity of barley; they will not [harvest it(?) ...]" (Simpson 2003: 446–7). Due to the anger of Re, dishonesty will prevail in this time of calamity, and social hierarchies will be reversed.[8] "Medes" will invade Egypt's borders, and eventually death will become so prevalent that animals will feed on exposed corpses. In a gesture toward hope, the lamb asserts that the time of troubles will be ameliorated by a king who will rule fifty-five years, following a repudiated king of two years. The true savior, however, will ascend the throne only after nine hundred years, when Re will (once again) sit as a uraeus upon the head of a pharaoh. After uttering the prophecy the lamb expired, and the pharaoh commanded that he be mummified (Figure 14).

Debates concerning the politics of the prophecy are too complex to address here, but the many chronicled misfortunes begin with a problematic flood and conclude with the restoration of divinely ordained royal rule, leading many scholars to suggest literary influence from *Neferti* (Blasius and Schipper 2002: 292; Thissen 2002: 126–7; Schipper 2014: 39–41). Given the text's similarities to the *Oracle of the Potter* (Section 3.1.4) – and given the choice of a lamb as

---

[7] The stele may have been influenced by a handbook for priests known from Roman Egypt that adopted a similar fictitious premise. A Second-Dynasty pharaoh, in the aftermath of a seven-year famine, received an exhortation in a dream to restore all the temples in the country. His command was published supposedly as decree in the temple at Heliopolis and later copied on a scroll (Quack 2012: 348–51).

[8] The Demotic *Instruction of Ankhsheshonq* states, "When Pre [*the sun god*] is angry with a land, he makes great its humble people and humbles its great people" (Lichtheim 1980: 164), a topic central to Chapter Four.

Figure 14 Roman ram mummy (MFA 72.4906) © 2023 Museum of Fine Arts, Boston

a mouthpiece for the sun god – some scholars speculate that priests of the ram god Khnum may have issued the oracle (Kákosy 1966: 345–6; Koenen 1970: 252; Simpson 2003: 445). Certainly, if Khnum were regarded as the likely instigator of famine, his priesthood would have had a vested interest in offering an explanation as well as hope for the future.

3.4 Oracle of the Potter (Known Anciently as Defense of a Potter to the King Amenophis)

According to its highly fragmentary frame narrative – written in Greek, but purportedly translated from a Demotic original – a potter journeys to the island of Helios/Re, perhaps at the command of Hermes/Thoth, to set up his workshop. Viewing him as committing a sacrilege, the locals smash his pots and drag him before King Amenophis. In defense of his actions, the potter launches into a prophecy. In this vision of the "future" an inadequate inundation leaves the land scorched and barren. Mention is made of the dimming of the sun, which, as with *Neferti*, is attributed to the divinity's willful withdrawal from the affairs of humankind (Kerkeslager 1998: 73, 78). The potter predicts:

> The land will not harmonize with the seeds. The majority of its things will be destroyed by the wind. [The fa]rmer will be demanded to pay taxes even for things which he did not sow, [and th]ey are fighting with one another in Egypt because the<y> are lacking in food supplies. For the things which they cultivate [another man w]ill reap. (Kerkeslager 1998: 73)

In the countryside there will be anarchy and flight, and "among pregnant women a curse and much death" (Kerkeslager 1998: 75). Civil war will break out among the Typhonian/Sethian Greeks, Egypt will be invaded by Syrians and Nubians, and Alexandria will be destroyed. Only then will the Nile return to a mark of plentitude. At that point, dead trees will revive, breezes will be orderly, and summer and winter will return to their proper cycles.

The oracle bears strong similarities to the other texts discussed in this section. Like *Neferti* and *Lamb*, it employs a framing narrative in which the prophecy is delivered before a king who lived many centuries prior to the events foreseen. It shares an emphasis on foreign infiltration with both texts and an alarmingly muted sun with *Neferti* (Koenen 1970: 251; Dunand 1977: 48–9; Bazzana 2018: 216–18). Convergences with *Lamb* are particularly close. The potter makes specific reference to the lamb's prediction that the short reign of a repudiated king will be followed by the fifty-five-year reign of a benevolent successor – this time designated as "of Helios." Both texts end with the abrupt death of the oracle-giver. Not surprisingly, the entity that possessed the island-dwelling potter is almost universally identified as Khnum, often designated as "Soul of Re," "Lord of Elephantine" and "of the Potter's Wheel." Khnum's role would link the text to the *Famine Stele* as well as to *Lamb*, as will be discussed in Section 3.2 (Kákosy 1966: 345–6, 351–2; Koenen 1970: 249; Bazzana 2018: 215–18).

Although *Potter* almost certainly "foretold" many of the same events as *Lamb*, the fact that neither the destruction of Alexandria nor the arrival of the long-awaited savior king had yet come to pass may have accounted for *Potter's* continuing popularity. The five surviving Greek manuscripts of *Potter* date to the second and third century CE, long after the "predicted" eastern invasions occurred. During recurrent famines, however, urban elites of Hellenistic heritage still dominated positions of power and imposed exorbitant taxes (Beyerle 2016: 174–5; Bazzana 2018: 211–14, 220–1). Interestingly, two recensions and an unpublished fragment from Oxyrhynchus add anti-Jewish sentiment to the oracular proclamation (Beyerle 2016: 174–5, 180–1). While this material may properly belong to the Ptolemaic version, the sentiments would presumably have resonated in the aftermath of the Jewish revolt of 115–117 CE during which Egyptian Jews attacked pagan temples. The crushing of this revolt was still celebrated annually in Hermopolis eighty years later, likely with the enthusiastic support of priesthoods such as Khnum's (Frankfurter 1992: 208–19; Blasius and Schipper 2002: 297).

Figure 15 Statuette of an Old Kingdom potter named Ny-kau-Inpu
(OIM 10628), courtesy of the Oriental Institute Museum
of the University of Chicago

3.5 Demotic Chronicle

The highly fragmentary third-century BCE papyrus on which the *Demotic Chronicle* is written possesses no beginning and no end. Almost assuredly, however, a framing narrative originally existed in which a medium prophesied before King Nectanebo I (c. 380–362). In the text, this king receives exhortations and oracles. He is, for example, compared to a gardener and commanded to water the bushes so that the trees might revive. According to the commentary, the statement indicated that the king should guard against greediness. Rampant corruption and plundering were particularly problematic, as his subjects hungered, and even the gods were suffering from radically reduced rations. Other oracular references were to farmers weeping due to an insufficient barley harvest. Desperate masses, the oracle predicted, will seek help from the high priest of Memphis but receive only starvation food (i.e., "that which is not cultivated to serve as nourishment"). Only with the arrival of foreigners would the Nile rise to its proper height and the people cease to hunger (Felber 2002: 87–9, 104–5).

Given that *Chronicle* seems to have been composed in the Ptolemaic Period, the textual elaboration concerning a drought long past seems gratuitous – unless its audience was meant to draw a parallel between the co-occurrence of famine and corrupt rulers in the past and the situation under the Ptolemies (Section 3.1.2). The overarching point of *Chronicle*, however, is its prediction of a savior king – an individual who would hail from Herakleopolis and be championed by yet another ram god, Harsaphes. If the oracles in question issued from a mouthpiece of Harsaphes, as would make sense given the content of the text and the god's formal and functional parallels to Khnum, László Kákosy's proposal that the Egyptians drew an interpretative connection between words for "ram" (*sr*) and "to predict" (*śr*) is of interest (Kákosy 1966: 353–5).

3.6 Prophecy from Tebtynis

A badly damaged second-century CE prophetic papyrus – written in Demotic and originally housed in the temple library of the crocodile deity Soknebtunis at Tebtunis – contains many familiar elements. A note written on the outside of the scroll suggests that it once possessed a frame story in which an individual on campaign had pitched camp in the east. There, he seems to have received a prophecy to the effect that the Nile flood will fail to nurture the land, resulting in substandard harvests. Social disorder and crime will accompany the ecological downturn. During this troubled time, people will neglect the gods, who will in turn neglect them, and Memphis and Alexandria will suffer harm. Eventually, evil will be vanished by a beneficent ruler who will restore the country's temples and its power in the world. Like *Potter*, which it closely resembles, the prophecy circulated in the second century CE. Its time of composition, however, remains a matter of speculation (Quack 2002: 254–63).

The long gap that separates the *Prophecy of Neferti* from others composed in the Greco-Roman period is puzzling. In Dynastic Egypt, deities were believed to make their wishes known through dreams or by directing the movements of the priests who carried their statue in procession. Every now and again, however, an allusion is made to prophecy, especially with reference to the famine in the First Intermediate Period. In the *Teaching for Merikare*, the political chaos of the time is said to have been "foretold" by ancestors (Simpson 2003: 159), while in the *Admonitions* of *Ipuwer* the sage mentions "things which were ordained for you in the age of Horus, in the time . . . " and "the prediction of the ancestors" (Enmarch 2008: 221–2). Although *Merikare* and *Ipuwer* could hypothetically refer to the prophecy attributed to Neferti, the dates of all three texts are hotly contested, and thus it is difficult to understand their order or influences. According to the Ramesside "eulogy of writers," Neferti and Khakheperreseneb were "sages who foretold the future, that which came forth from their mouths took place" (Simpson 2003: 1), and Khakheperreseneb himself asserts, "I have said these things just as I have seen, beginning with the first generation down to those who shall come afterward, when they (too) shall imitate the past" (Simpson 2003: 212).

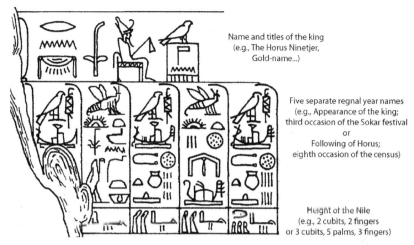

Name and titles of the king
(e.g., The Horus Ninetjer,
Gold-name...)

Five separate regnal year names
(e.g., Appearance of the king;
third occasion of the Sokar festival
or
Following of Horus;
eighth occasion of the census)

Height of the Nile
(e.g., 2 cubits, 2 fingers
or 3 cubits, 5 palms, 3 fingers)

Figure 16 Section of the annals on the Palermo Stone (after Nephiliskos, German Wikipedia), Creative Commons https://upload.wikimedia.org/ wikipedia/commons/e/e8/Palermo1.png https://de.wikipedia.org/wiki/Benutzer:Nephiliskos

Khakheperreseneb was said to be a *wab*-priest of Heliopolis and Neferti a Heliopolitan lector priest of Bastet (Parkinson 2002: 196–7, 200; Simpson 2003: 212, 215). If men of their vocation did occasionally prophesize in real life, it is worth noting that they would have had access to records that kept track of Nile flood levels in tandem with political events, like those used to compile the Memphite Palermo Stone (Figure 16). The correlations in such records between long stretches of erratic floods and the onset of political instability would be easy to recognize. Promoting the idea of famine as punishment may also have proved tempting for religious authorities. In a world in which gods animated nature, famines did not simply appear at random; they occurred due to a deity's displeasure and were ameliorated when divine anger had been placated. Severe famines and their attendant epidemics reliably resulted in widespread death and suffering, which lent a prophecy urgency. A prediction that a famine would occur in the indefinite future constituted the safest of bets, as did the prediction that the righting of wrongs in the natural and political worlds would co-occur. Plentiful harvests are, after all, a prerequisite for a stable state.

Despite these early references to prophets and prophecy in the pharaonic sources, *Neferti* remains the only work in which famine is closely tied to politics. Moreover, aside from a mention of the sun god having "withdrawn himself from men" (Simpson 2003: 218), the role of the divine is left unexplained. To understand why a prophetic tradition that weaponized famine surfaced in the first millennium BCE, it proves useful to explore both culture contact and climate.

3.7 Prophetic Narratives in Ptolemaic Egypt Likely Benefited from a Long Cross-Fertilization with Jewish Tradition

Before the Ptolemies, but well after the composition of *Neferti*, three Old Testament prophets – Isaiah, Jeremiah, and Ezekiel – purportedly tied divine displeasure to low Niles and sociopolitical chaos. The earliest, Isaiah, was said to have lived in the second half of the eighth century BCE, during a time when Assyrian and Egyptian armies were both active in Judah. The content of his prophecy is reminiscent of *Neferti* but also of Assyrian royal inscriptions and Exodus 1–15 (Aster 2015: 453). Yahweh – as channeled by Isaiah, molded by biblical authors, and redacted by editors – makes the promise: "I will stir up Egyptian against Egyptian – brother will fight against brother, neighbor against neighbor" (Isaiah 19:2). To ensure this happens, he vows to interfere with the inundation.

> The waters of the river will dry up, and the riverbed will be parched and dry. The canals will stink; the streams of Egypt will dwindle and dry up. The reeds and rushes will wither, also the plants along the Nile, at the mouth of the river. Every sown field along the Nile will become parched, will blow away and be no more . . . . [A]ll the wage earners will be sick at heart . . . The LORD will strike Egypt with a plague. (Isaiah 19:2, 6–7, 10, 22)

Despite these terrible predictions, Isaiah states that God will in the end show mercy – thanks in part to the devoted appeals from inhabitants of the City of the Sun, who speak Canaanite and swear loyalty to Yahweh. Isaiah's prophecy, with its emphasis on the "City of the Sun" (Heliopolis), has led Bernd Schipper to argue that the editors of the Septuagint altered the passage so that it might serve to counteract the anti-Semitism of certain recensions of the *Oracle of the Potter* (Schipper 2014: 49). Egyptian and Assyrian military activity in Canaan did, however, likely lead to the establishment of expatriate Jewish communities in Egypt. Many Jews likely arrived as refugees, but still more, taken as prisoners of war, would have been offered the traditional option of escaping slavery by enrolling in the Egyptian army. In the Late Period, most thriving Jewish communities were demonstrably military in origin (Modrzejewski 1997: 22–6).

According to First Isaiah, a Jewish king sanctioned by God would eventually recover the Jewish communities in diaspora – including those "from Egypt, from Patrôs, from Cush" – and bring them back to the promised land (Isaiah 11:11). Although the rest of Isaiah's prophecy fits well within an Old Testament tradition, scholars have long noted that these passages betray an unusual familiarity with Egyptian language and phraseology. The thick description of Nile flood failure, the wrongs done by foreign invaders, the positive invocation of a city of the sun, and the role of God in installing a savior king bear marked similarities to *Neferti*, *Potter*, and *Tebtynis* (Schipper 2014: 35–50).[9]

When Jeremiah and Ezekiel prophesied in the late seventh century BCE, it was Neo-Babylonian rather than Assyrian armies that occupied Canaan and menaced Egypt. Jeremiah is forced to flee Judea when his comrades assassinate the Neo-Babylonian governor. Upon arriving in Egypt and finding a robust resident Jewish population worshipping foreign deities in addition to Yahweh, Jeremiah relays a divine curse against the Nile Valley and "all the Jews living in the land of Egypt, those who were living in Migdol, Tahpanhes, Memphis, and the land of Patrôs" (Jeremiah 44:1). Concerning Migdol, Tahpanhes, and Memphis, all of which housed important garrisons during the Late Period, Jeremiah channels his god and vows, "I will take away the remnant of Judah who were determined to go to Egypt to settle there. They will all perish in Egypt; they will fall by the sword or die from famine . . . . I will punish those who live in Egypt with the sword, famine and plague, as I punished Jerusalem" (Jeremiah 44:12–13). The Neo-Babylonian victories foreseen by Jeremiah and Ezekiel never came true. At the time they were supposedly uttered, however, the ultimate success of the Neo-Babylonian armies must have been deemed only a matter of time. Yahweh's invocation of Jewish communities in Egypt is again notable and demonstrates that the priests in Jerusalem found their existence troubling.

The prophesied victory of Nebuchadnezzar over Egypt in the early sixth century, according to Ezekiel, would co-occur with a terrible drought. Using language of "woe and abomination," which resonates with Isaiah 19 and *Lamb* (Simpson 2003: 446), Ezekiel speaks for God, saying, "[A]nd the land of Egypt shall be a desolation and a waste. Then they will know that I am the LORD. Because you said, 'The Nile is mine, and I made it,' therefore, behold, I am against you and against your streams, and I will make the land of Egypt an utter waste and desolation, from Migdol to Aswan (lit. Syene), as far as the border of Cush" (Ezekiel 29:9–10). In Ezekiel 30:12–18, Yahweh promises to "dry up the Nile" and – through the medium of Nebuchadnezzar – to bring devastation on Patrôs, Memphis, Pelusium, Tahpanhes, Heliopolis, and other sites known or presumed to have housed garrisons. In a conciliatory gesture, however, he promises that forty years after Nebuchadnezzar's destruction, he will "bring back the captives of Egypt and cause them to return to the land of Patrôs, to the land of their origin" (Ezekiel 29:14).

---

[9] The emphasis on the suffering of wage laborers during a famine is similar both to *Ipuwer* and to various chronicles of Medieval and Ottoman famines (Morris 2020: 240).

God's choice to smite Egypt with famine, pestilence, and war is not surprising, but the fact that all three prophets mention Patrôs (Egyptian *Pa-ta-rsy* or "The Southern Land") – never otherwise encountered as a toponym in the Old Testament – is. In Egyptian texts, the toponym referred to the southernmost region of Egypt, extending at times from Thebes in the north to the First Cataract in the south (Porten 1968: 42–3, 176; Quack 2021). Given that Patrôs in these contexts, as Isaiah 11:11 specifies, lay at the juncture between Egypt and Nubian Kush, a locale in the First Cataract would make sense. The presence of a thriving Jewish community on the island of Elephantine, which archival records indicate was in regular communication with Jews elsewhere in Egypt and with temple authorities in Jerusalem, renders such an identification doubly attractive. As noted earlier, in each of these prophetic texts Patrôs appears in tandem with established communities of Jewish garrison soldiers, namely at Migdol, Tahpanhes (the fortress of Daphne, modern Tell Defenneh), and likely also Heliopolis (located close to Memphis).

The date of the foundation of the Jewish community at Elephantine is unclear, but it was likely established in the Twenty-sixth Dynasty (c. 664–525). The Saite kings, having begun as vassals of the Assyrians, fought against Neo-Babylonian armies and routinely utilized foreign troops to solidify their grip on power. Following Nebuchadnezzar's destruction of the temple at Jerusalem, they evidently granted the community at Elephantine rights to build their own temple to Yahweh, which was left unharmed when the Persians invaded Egypt and placed the garrison under their charge. Aramaic archives discovered in the houses of community members indicate that the garrison inhabitants corresponded with relatives in Syene, with other Jewish enclaves in Egypt, and with the re-established priesthood in Jerusalem under Persian rule (Porten 1968: 8–15). It is therefore virtually certain that the Jewish community at Elephantine would have been familiar with the prophetic practice of men like Jeremiah. The temple of Yahweh was the only authorized Jewish temple outside Jerusalem. Given that it was situated directly across the street from a sacred precinct of Khnum – the god at whose command the Nile rose or fell – the missing link between *Neferti* and the Greco-Roman prophecies, discussed earlier, should almost certainly be sought in Elephantine (c. 525–404; Figure 17).

The relationship between the priesthood of Khnum and the neighboring Jewish community deteriorated in the reign of Darius II (c. 410 BCE), due perhaps to the Jewish temple's perceived encroachment into shared space. Before that time, however, community members enjoyed peaceful relations for well over a century. Intermarriage between Jews and their neighbors seems to have been unremarkable. The second husband of a well-documented Jewish woman, for instance, was Egyptian, and she swore an oath in a court case

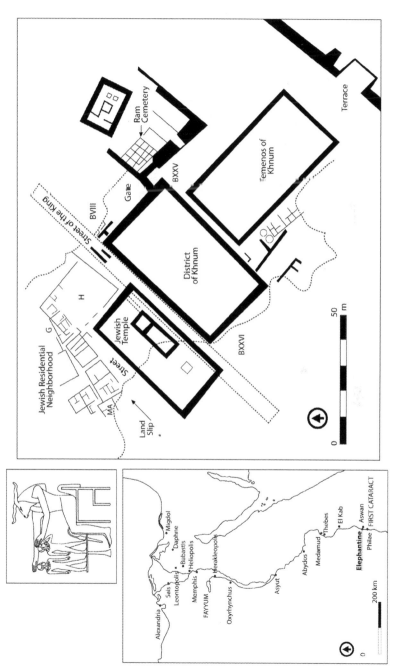

Figure 17 The god Khnum and the townsite of Elephantine (Redrawn by Riva Weinstein after Frankfort 1978: figure 23; Rosenberg 2004: 9 (based on von Pilgrim 1999: figure 17), both images © University of Chicago Press)

by Khnum's wife Satet. A man named Ananiah, who held a position of responsibility within Yahweh's temple, likewise married an Egyptian (Porten 1968: 153, 201–13, 245–55).

While the Jewish garrison may have been decommissioned following the expulsion of the Persian kings, long-standing ties with their Egyptian kin and neighbors make it likely that many families remained on or near Elephantine and continued practicing their religion. New waves of Jewish immigrants to Egypt in the early Ptolemaic Period perhaps strengthened their numbers and revivified their faith. While Khnum's perceived agency over the Nile flood is perhaps enough to explain his association with Ptolemaic prophecies of famine, the similarity of these utterances to the fire-and-brimstone predictions of Old Testament prophets – and the lack of a politically potent prophetic tradition in Egypt prior to this period of cultural mixing – suggests that the ram-god's status as a spoken-word environmental prophet may have owed something to Yahweh.

3.8 How Effective Was Prophecy at Serving as an Unwitting Host for the Curation of Social Memories of Famine in Egypt?

The descriptions of Nile flood failure and famine in Egyptian prophetic writings contain information about many of the most salient features of Nilotic famines known from historical records. Low floods and drought, often accompanied by high winds, resulted in poor harvests. Governments were unable to maintain order and sometimes fell to outside invaders. Gods and humans suffered from hunger. Crime was rampant, hierarchies were overthrown, angst and violence cleaved the closest of ties, and many died from famine, pestilence, or social turmoil.

While famine narratives can admittedly appear bland in brief summation, specific details occasionally suggest either first-hand knowledge or knowledge that had been curated in social memory. *Neferti* and *Potter*, for example, both describe a dramatic solar dimming. According to Neferti's prophecy,

> The sun is obscured and gives no light that men may see. Men cannot live when stormclouds hover, and all are stunned in its absence . . . . As for Re, he has withdrawn himself from men. He will rise at the appointed time, but none will know when noon has come. None will behold his shadow, none will rejoice when he is seen. No longer will the eyes stream with water, for he will be in the sky only like the moon. (Simpson 2003: 216, 218–19)

The potter predicted, similarly, "the sun will become dim because it does not want to see the evils in Egypt" (Kerkeslager 1998: 73). The brief veiling of the sun during sandstorms would not have merited note. Solar dimming, however, is specifically mentioned in other accounts of ecological downturn. Ankhtifi of

Mo'Alla, for instance, boasted that he had taken care of his town in the First Intermediate Period, when "the sky was clouded and the earth [was parched (?) and when everybody died] of hunger on this sandbank of Apophis" (Seidlmayer 2000: 129). A prayer to Amun, likely penned during a troubled year in the late Nineteenth Dynasty, provides a New Kingdom parallel. The author addresses Amun with the plea, "Come to me, Amun, and save me in this wretched year. It has come about that the sun rises not; winter is come in the summer" (Caminos 1954: 171).

Solar dimming occurred in conjunction with terrible famines in the Ptolemaic and Roman periods as well. In 44 BCE the sun was dimmed by a veil of volcanic dust, an event later interpreted by writers, including Virgil and Ovid, as either a portent or a consequence of Caesar's murder. According to Plutarch,

> ... [A]ll that year its orb rose pale and without radiance, while the heat that came down from it was slight and ineffectual, so that the air in its circulation was dark and heavy owing to the feebleness of the warmth that penetrated it, and the fruits, imperfect and half ripe, withered away and shriveled up on account of the coldness of the atmosphere. (Plutarch, *Life of Caesar* 69.4)

Like Neferti, Marc Anthony interpreted the sun's apparent diminishment as divine displeasure, stating that "the very sun turned away, as if it too were loath to look upon the foul deed against Caesar" (Hillard 2010: 209; McConnell et al. 2020: 15443–7). The following year, as volcanic emissions suppressed Ethiopia's monsoons, Egypt was wracked with famine.

Reports of a startlingly weakened sun abounded in the third century CE as well. Writing from Carthage in the 240s, Cyprian observed, "The summer sun burns less bright over the fields of grain. The temperance of spring is no longer for rejoicing, and the ripening fruit does not hang from autumn trees" (Harper 2017: 130). Cyprian's observations, Kyle Harper notes, are verified by contemporary beryllium isotope records. The decade also witnessed a succession of insufficient floods that resulted in massive inflation and, in 248 CE, left the Nile as parched as the desert (Harper 2017: 131, 134).

These prophetic writings are also striking in that they draw attention to the suffering of farmers at the hands of rapacious tax collectors. Neferti predicts, "The land is destitute, although its rulers are numerous; it is ruined, but its taxes are immense. Sparse is the grain, but great is the measure" (Simpson 2003: 218). Likewise in *Potter*, an account of a poor harvest is followed by the statement "[The fa]rmer will be demanded to pay taxes even for things which he did not sow, [and th]ey are fighting with one another in Egypt because th<ey> are lacking in food supplies. For the things which they cultivate [another man w]ill reap" (Kerkeslager 1998: 73). Finally, if Robert Ritner's translation of an enigmatic portion of the *Famine Stele* is correct, peasants who could not pay their taxes sought asylum within temple walls: "Grain was scarce, the kernels dried out, everything edible in short supply. Every man was so restrained by his taxation that they went inside so as not to go out" (Simpson 2003: 387). Certainly, attempts by governments to extract a nonexistent surplus from taxpayers have likely accounted for more rebellions, insurrections, and civil unrest than any other catalyst in the Egyptian historical record (Dunand 1977: 64; al-Maqrīzī 1994: 11; Blouin 2014: 254–97; Manning 2018: 167–72).

If the details of some prophesied famines seem authentic, it may be because prophecies most often "predicted" ecological downturns that were already in progress or had occurred within living memory. While the date of *Neferti* is unclear, Jan Assmann suggests that the text co-arose with lamentation literature in the wake of the First Intermediate Period and that the genre lay dormant until a similar constellation of famines, civil war, and weak rulers arose in the Ptolemaic Period (Assmann 2003: 109). Prophecies of doom are most compelling in the midst of actual chaos. That said, *Neferti*'s inclusion in the New Kingdom scribal curriculum may have usefully served to embed its description of famine dynamics into the social memory of future administrators.

For a fabricated prophecy to be deemed a conduit for social memory, it does not matter whether it was written in a time of scarcity or plenty. What matters is that it was *consumed* in a time of plenty. The *Famine Stele, Prophecy of the Lamb, Oracle of the Potter,* and *Demotic Chronicle* were all written or had recensions circulating in the highly turbulent mid-to-late Ptolemaic Period (Kákosy 1966: 345, 355; Blasius and Schipper 2002: 296–7; Simpson 2003: 445). During this era, volcanic eruptions worldwide dimmed the sun and their emissions depressed monsoon rainfall in Ethiopia, radically reducing the Nile's flow on numerous occasions. The first major eruption in this period occurred late in the reign of Ptolemy II (c. 247 BCE) and was soon followed by the first of many famines and revolts. The correlation between volcanic eruptions and low Nile floods is greater than 98 percent, and eight of the nine documented periods of social unrest appear to have coincided with these eruptions (Manning 2018: 135–7; 158–72). The *Famine Stele* and the prophecies – with their allusions to specific kings, civil strife, and invasions – instrumentalized contemporary famines for political purposes.

Predictions like those purportedly uttered by the lamb or the potter, which were recopied and occasionally reworked in the Roman Period, and which offered ongoing hope for a distant salvation, *did* have the potential to act as vehicles for social memory, depending on when they were received. *Lamb* was mentioned by many ancient authors, but the sole surviving copy dates to 4 CE. While memories of Nilotic famines from the reign of Cleopatra surely still circulated, no known famines occurred at that time. The existing copies of *Potter*, on the other hand, date to the second and third century CE. Disasters during this fraught era include famines and violent country-wide revolts of the Jewish population in the reigns of Trajan and Hadrian, continuing famines in the reign of Antonius Pius, as well as rebellions, famines, and plagues in the reigns of Marcus Aurelius and Commodus – all before the onset of the famously turbulent third century. It is pertinent that around 150 CE Egypt was emerging from the Roman Climate Optimum, a process that resulted in substantially increased incidences of drought, famine, and disease (Harper 2017: 39–64, 98–159). The problem with prophecies as effective conduits for social memories of famine, then, is that they attain peak interest and believability only when the specter of an analogous event looms large.

During hard times, *Potter* appears to have been dusted off and regarded with renewed relevancy and hope, for it offered a narrative template in which famine, violence, and suffering would be followed by salvation from a figure associated with the sun. The prophecy in this respect is thought by many to have influenced the Jewish Third Sibylline Oracle, *Apocalypse of Asclepius*, and *Apocalypse of Elijah* (Dunand 1977; Frankfurter 1993; Collins 1997; Quack 2016). Although this rich body of literature cannot be considered here, it is notable that as the envisioned chaos became increasingly apocalyptic, the descriptions of Nile flood failure tilted toward the surreal.

Perhaps the most significant divide in this corpus of Egyptian writing is whether the savior (or his dynasty) existed in the present and the demons in the past, as in *Prophecy of Neferti*, or the demons existed in the present and the savior in the future, as in the case of the Greco-Roman prophecies. Court authors were well served by denigrating the past and promoting the present. Priestly authors, on the other hand, may have been inclined to save salvation for an undefined future so as to keep faith alive and revenues flowing. As in the case of the anonymized cartouches that often decorated temple walls in Greco-Roman Egypt, the identity of the savior king hardly mattered (Figure 18). That the king-to-come was seen to be committed to the priesthood, however, was crucial.

4 The Role of Rituals in Preserving Social Memory

This Element asks how ancient Egyptians endeavored to remember famine in the midst of a life filled with feasts. Listening to stories passed down through the generations, consulting written narratives, and taking prophetic warnings seriously were all available options. Each, however, encountered a similar

Figure 18 Cartouches on Kalabsha Temple, Nubia, filled with the title
"pharaoh," Creative Commons (photograph by Iris Fernandez, Ancient
World Image Bank) www.flickr.com/photos/isawnyu/5913199610

challenge: accounts of famine may interest survivors and (occasionally) their
children or grandchildren, but most generate significant attention only when
a similar threat appears imminent.

In *Religion and Cultural Memory*, Jan Assmann asserts that Jewish tradition
was effectively unique in antiquity in developing specific mnemonic techniques
to incorporate past trauma into social memory. He highlights seven strategies:
rote learning, educational and conversational remembering, making visible
through body marking or door posts, publication, oral transmission via songs
or poetry, canonization of the covenant, and festivals of collective remembering
(Assmann 2006: 16–20). To what extent might ancient Egyptians have
attempted to maintain vigilance against severe famines by drawing on such
memory aides? The texts considered thus far were certainly composed and
copied, some were studied in school, and most might have begun their life as
performances or songs. Ipuwer's purported profession as an overseer of
singers – and the statement credited to him that musicians sang dirges in
a time of famine – suggests that, as in modern Ethiopia, song may well have
been an important medium for the communication of suffering (Enmarch 2008:
226). Songs of lamentation, however, can be as ephemeral as the events that

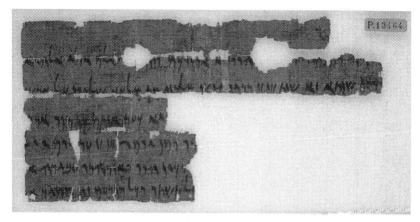

Figure 19 Letter sent to the Jewish garrison at Elephantine concerning the Passover Festival, 419 BCE (Berlin, ÄMP P. 13464, recto.), © bpk Bildagentur/Ägyptisches Museum, Berlin /Art Resource, NY

inspired them. Fekade Azeze, for example, discovered that most individuals who had composed songs or poems during the terrible Ethiopian famine of 1984–1985 had forgotten them a decade later (Azeze 1998: 28–9).

This final section asserts that in Egypt an annual festival of remembrance proved most successful at keeping the worst-case scenario of famine fresh in the collective consciousness. In making this case, it is useful to first consider the long-standing and crucial role of festivals of remembrance in Jewish tradition. In Egypt in antiquity, Jews celebrated festivals that encoded the hard truth that even under friendly regimes or kings, their religion rendered them vulnerable to persecution. In Elephantine in the late fifth century BCE, Jewish garrison soldiers and their families celebrated Passover (Porten 1968: 128–33; Figure 19). Additionally, the Third Book of Maccabees states that in the mid-to-late Ptolemaic Period the Jewish community "partook of a banquet of deliverance" and "days of joyfulness" that celebrated a story of survival (3 Maccabees 7:18–19). According to this narrative, Ptolemy IV (221–204) – angered at having been denied entrance to the Jewish temple in Jerusalem while on campaign – had attempted to execute Egypt's Jewish community using intoxicated war elephants. The festival celebrated the divine intervention that ensured his failure.

The Jewish historian Josephus discusses a variant of this festival still celebrated in the early second century CE. It commemorated the succession of miracles that saved Egyptian Jews from the wrath of a king named Ptolemy who had intended to utilize drunken elephants to kill them (Josephus, *Against Apion* II, 5). Both the backstory and the identity of the murderous Ptolemy, however, differed. Thus, for the sake of the festival, *why* the Jewish people got in trouble did not matter – they were innocent of wrongdoing in both cases. What mattered was that they had been threatened but ultimately saved by God.

A wry Jewish joke contends that many of the religion's most important festivals can be summarized in three short sentences: "They tried to kill us. They didn't succeed. Let's eat!" The Festival of the Elephants, Passover, Hanukkah, and Purim are all festivals of remembrance in which specific catalysts matter less than the frighteningly close brush with genocide. It is this vulnerability that must be inculcated. What Assmann does not discuss is that the success of these festivals may be largely ascribed to the fact that their somber and disheartening message was counterbalanced by "days of joyfulness." The pleasure for adults often involved permission to imbibe an unusual amount. So too, the celebrants encouraged the enthusiastic participation of children by serving special festival foods, singing songs, and providing opportunities to dress up, play games, and/or receive gifts. It is tempting to surmise that drunken elephants may well have served in the "days of joyfulness" as a pretext for adults to drink and for children to imitate the clumsy, lumbering beasts who, in fact, managed to hurt only the bad Ptolemaic soldiers.

According to Assmann, rituals of connective memory that incorporate tales of past *but potentially recurrent* suffering – so prominent in Jewish tradition – did not exist in pharaonic or Greco-Roman Egypt (Assmann 2006: 16, 54). This section argues against his assertion. It maintains that the specter of severe famine was kept vivid in Egypt through the annual celebration of the New Year, one of the few festivals celebrated throughout the country. Like its Jewish counterparts, this festival embedded the hard truths that famines impose extreme suffering, shred the social fabric, and cause unimaginable mortality in a festival that both acknowledged these dangers and celebrated the divine intervention that would hopefully continue to divert them.

4.1 The Nile Festival Likely Began with an Invitation to Meditate on the Terrors of a Severe Famine

Like many of the most successful communal rituals, the New Year's festival gained much of its potency by juxtaposing sorrow and sobriety with delight and drunkenness. At the pivotal point in the natural cycle that marked the New Year, an infusion of joy was sorely needed. The Nile had retreated to its lowest levels, and the annual plague had claimed a lion's share of its victims. The five days that directly preceded the New Year were viewed as the most dangerous and ill-omened days in the Egyptian calendar (Borghouts 1978: 12–14; Leitz 1994: 416–27; Pinch 1994: 38–9; Gnirs 2015: 126, 129–30).[10]

---

[10] For Christian and Muslim parallels for the New Year being associated with the arrival of the flood waters and the banishing of the plague, see Mikhail 2017: 182.

During these five days, communities all along the Nile seem to have been invited to contemplate the disasters that would befall them should the river fail to rise. A hymn to the inundation god Hapi, almost certainly composed in the Twelfth Dynasty and likely performed in ceremonies at the start of the New Year (Hagen 2013: 89; Jansen-Winkeln 2017: 121), demonstrates how priests invoked the horrors of famine in a ritual context. The hymn describes the inundation god's power:

> Maker of barley, creator of emmer. He lets the temples celebrate. When he is sluggish noses clog. Everyone is poor. As the sacred loaves are pared, a million perish among men. When he plunders, the whole land rages. Great and small roar . . . . If he is heavy, the people dwindle. A year's food supply is lost. The rich man looks concerned, Everyone is seen with weapons. Friend does not attend to friend. Cloth is wanting for one's clothes. Noble children lack their finery. (Lichtheim 1975: 206–8)

In tandem with the literature and prophetic texts discussed in prior sections, this hymn identifies the distinctive characteristics of a severe famine as civil strife, mass mortality, and the destabilization of social hierarchy (Luria 1929: 408; Blasius and Schipper 2002: 284–5, 288).

During these five epagomenal days, pessimistic literature may have been mobilized alongside hymns to stress the destructive power of famine. Ludwig Morenz noted that the verso of *Admonitions of Ipuwer* (P. Leiden I 344) contained hymns to deities – including one in which Amun is identified with Hapi, Khnum, and the solar father of the Distant Goddess, discussed in Section 4.4. On this basis, he suggested that *Ipuwer* and the other texts with which it was found – including spells to ward off dangers on the epagomenal days – would have been performed during festivals in which it was crucial that order vanquish chaos (Morenz 1999: 131–2; Zandee 1992: 1087, 1093–5). Salomo Luria (1929) argued much the same. The inversions of social hierarchy invoked in *Ipuwer*, he noted, would fit seamlessly into a great many carnivalesque festivals in which social hierarchies are briefly upended (Luria 1929: 406, 421).

The thrust of the numerous and varied inversions in *Ipuwer*, in other pessimistic texts, and in prophecies can be encapsulated by two characteristic observations. First, traditional power relations are reversed (e.g., "the one who gives commands is (now) the one to whom commands are given" and vice versa).[11] Second, nobility and wealth are no longer synonymous

---

[11] The *Lamentations of Khakheperreseneb*, Simpson 2003: 213. See also *Ipuwer*, Enmarch 2008: 223, 225–6, 228, 230, 232; *Neferti*, Simpson 2003, 219; the *Prophecy of the Lamb*, Simpson 2003: 446; the *Oracle of the Potter*; Kerkeslager 1998: 76. According to P. Oxy. 2554, a fragmentary astrological prophecy not discussed in the previous chapter, famine, sickness,

(e.g., "the poor of the land have become the wealthy, and he who owned property (now) has nothing."[12] As Ipuwer observes, invoking Khnum perhaps, "the land spins round as does a potter's wheel" (Enmarch 2008: 223).

Because these inversions – deemed both formulaic and hyperbolic – come to the fore especially strongly in *Ipuwer*, this text, more than any other, has been dismissed as irrelevant for understanding Egypt's social history (e.g., Lichtheim 1975: 149–50; Parkinson 2002: 207; Enmarch 2008: 64). In challenging the prevailing scholarly bias, this section argues four main points. First, famines *do* often spark profound shifts in social power and wealth. Second, elites facing similar situations have historically drawn upon the trope of social inversion to dehumanize the formerly poor and satirize their ambitions as outsized and against nature. Third, after invoking the scarier ramifications of famine, participants in the New Year's festival utilized inversion and incongruity to showcase its more "comical" consequences. And, finally, the rites of reversal presented in the course of the festival were likely to have been popular and long-lived precisely because they could be interpreted differently by different social classes.

4.2 Famines Have Often Sparked Profound Shifts in Social Power and Wealth

Cross-cultural studies demonstrate that three broad mechanisms tend to facilitate income redistribution during and after severe famines: crime, revolution, and high mortality rates. Steep spikes in the price of food during famines characteristically result in surges of larceny. In the texts considered in Sections 2 and 3, theft is repeatedly stated to have run rampant, an observation that finds support in Medieval and Ottoman accounts.[13] During the Great Famine in Ireland, rates of burglary and theft quintupled, and upward of seventeen thousand citizens were arrested on similar charges in a span of fifteen months during the siege of Leningrad, discussed in Section 2 (Ó Gráda 2009: 53; Peri 2017: 143). Similarly, sharp spikes in grain prices and a pronounced uptick in tomb robbery characterized much of Egypt's late Twentieth Dynasty. Pharaonic authorities tracking ill-gotten gains most often found robbers by seeking out commoners living above their means – buying slaves or having

---

and war will result in a rapid turnover of kings, "and the poor will be exalted and the rich humbled" (Rea 1966: 81).

[12] *Ipuwer*, Enmarch 2008: 229–32; *Neferti*, Simpson 2003: 218–19; *Lamb*, Simpson 2003: 446.

[13] *Dispute between a Man and His Ba, Ipuwer, Prophecy from Tebtynis, Demotic Chronicle*, and *Famine Stele* (Simpson 2003: 184–5; Enmarch 2008: 221–3, 226–7, 231; Quack 2002: 256; Felber 2002: 88; Morris 2020: 237–8).

access to suspicious quantities of silver. One woman, in her own defense, stated that she had obtained her silver "in exchange for barley in the year of the hyenas when there was a famine" (Peet 1930: 153). Only in a time characterized by severe hunger could this defense and others like it appear even remotely plausible. Reports in besieged Leningrad of cafeteria and bakery workers sporting fur coats and jewelry provide a more contemporary parallel (Kochina 2014: 60; Peri 2017: 144–5).

The line between robbing the rich for profit and robbing the rich to right social wrongs is difficult to discern at a distance, but it was no doubt convenient that the two goals could be neatly wrapped into one. Historical records demonstrate that inefficient, inattentive, or avaricious elites typically served as lightning rods for discontent during ecological downturns. Perceived abuses of the social contract that bound a government to its people also provoked widespread anger and demonstrations (al-Maqrīzī 1994: 30; Sabra 2000: 144, 155; Mikhail 2011: 217–18). In the *Teaching for Merikare* references to an agitated populace are frequent (Simpson 2003: 153–5). So too, Ipuwer reports that "every town says, 'Let's drive out the strong among us!'" Storehouses and government offices were said to be raided: "[S]cribes of the field-register, their writings have been obliterated; the life-grain of Egypt is a free-for-all. O, yet the rulings of the labour enclosure are cast (lit. put) out, and one walks on th in the alleys; wretches tear them up in the streets." Even more alarming, "[T]hings have been done which have not been done before, having come <to> the removal of the king by wretches . . . . For look, it has come to impoverishing the land of kingship by a few people who are ignorant of counsels! For look, it has come to rebellion against the strong uraeus of Re' which pacified the Two lands" (Enmarch 2008: 223, 228–9).

Although the dates of these texts are admittedly unclear, the aftermath of mob violence may well be visible in the archaeological record, as attested by the selective torching of the late-Sixth-Dynasty governor's palace at 'Ain Asil in Dakhla Oasis, by the disordered corpses of over thirty-five people recovered beneath burnt heaps of rubble outside a late-Old-Kingdom temple platform at Mendes, and by the scorched ruins of the Old Kingdom–First Intermediate Period granary complex, storerooms, and other remains at Kom Ombo (Soukiassian 1997: 16–17; Redford 2010: 46–50; Forstner-Müller et al. 2019: 67–70).

When revolutions succeed, the class of people who most directly benefited from the regime is often ousted from authority along with the ruler. Thus, the lineages and regional centers that grew to greatest prominence in Egypt's Intermediate Periods tended to be new to power. In the wake of the famine's many political consequences, then, the old guard elite must have felt the poor had indeed become rich and the rich poor. To Egyptologists such as Adolf Erman and Boris Turayev who had themselves lived through political revolutions, the inversions that characterize *Ipuwer* felt freshly resonant (Luria 1929: 413–14). As Max Pieper wrote in 1928, *Ipuwer* gave the impression of "a Bolshevik revolution in ancient Egypt ... as if everything was turned topsy-turvy, precisely like in the past couple of years" (quoted in Schneider 2017: 312).

The social processes triggered by the ecological downturn at the end of the Old Kingdom, as well as the other factors that led to the collapse of the central government, did result in social leveling. When regional rulers began to enlarge their territory, the burial monuments they erected were scarcely more impressive than those of their followers. Most have remained archaeologically invisible. Conversely, the graves of commoners were generally larger and better equipped than they had been at any time since the imposition of dynastic rule (Seidlmayer 2000: 122). While this leveling may have been due to an elimination or reduction in taxes, it almost certainly evinced a renewed societal interest in elaborate burial rites.

Mortuary expenditure has been shown cross-culturally to escalate in tandem with shifts in society that enable social movement among classes. Thus, at points when one's position was no longer ascribed from cradle to grave – when by dint of hard work and creative maneuvering one could, in fact, move up the social ladder – people eager to aggrandize have found competitive feasting and displays to be well worth the expenditure (Morris 2006: 62–3). Little wonder, then, that the upper classes grew increasingly alarmed, both at the financial resources available to commoners and at the boldness with which they advertised their new status as consumers.

Finally, the economic shifts that occurred in the wake of mass mortality likely also convinced hereditary elites that the poor had profited. The worst of Egypt's Medieval and Ottoman famines resulted in astounding death tolls from starvation and from diseases that run rampant once immune systems are compromised by malnutrition (al-Baghdādī 1965: 55 *l*, 65 *l*; al-Maqrīzī 1994: 3, 11, 31, 45–6; Sabra 2000: 144, 152, 154, 157–9). The virulent plague that struck between 1790 and 1796 CE in tandem with a long streak of famine, for example, not only killed Egypt's leader but also, according to historian Alan Mikhail,

> successors immediately rose to power only to die themselves three days later. Those who replaced them also died in the course of a few days .... Leaders came to power in the morning and died by late afternoon .... Many large Cairene families were decimated by the plague. (Mikhail 2008: 255–6)

The flight of the rich in the wake of famine and plague – remarked upon by Ipuwer and by the potter in his prophecy – has historically resulted in the abandonment of a great deal of property (Enmarch 2008: 231; Kerkeslager 1998: 75). After the famine of 1199 to 1201 CE, Egypt's richest estates were for the most part deserted due to the death or flight of their inhabitants (al-Baghdādī 1965: 64 *l*). Likewise, due to the high mortality during the famine and plague of 1791, the official or unofficial seizure of possessions from people who fled or died was said to have offered a unique opportunity for enrichment (Mikhail 2011: 224).

The social effects of severe plagues on the societies that emerged from them are perhaps best known from records of the Black Death, which hit Europe and the Middle East in successive waves during the fourteenth century CE. Reports suggest that, for some survivors, the plague's aftermath proved a boon. As Barbara Tuchman writes,

> With a glut of merchandise on the shelves for too few customers, prices at first plunged and survivors indulged in a wild orgy of spending. The poor moved into empty houses, slept on beds, and ate off silver. Peasants acquired unclaimed tools and livestock, even a wine press, forge, or mill left without owners, and other possessions they never had before.[14] (Tuchman 1978: 117)

In the aftermath of such massive loss of life, survivors were in a unique position to claim abandoned or inherited property, and the plight of the poor seems also to have improved due to a scarcity of manpower.

Ipuwer may indirectly reference such a newly urgent demand for laborers when he says, "O, yet the Inundation rises (but) no one ploughs" (Enmarch 2008: 222). His observation anticipates al-Maqrīzī's, with respect to the famine of 1199 to 1201 that "when God succored His creatures through the flooding of the Nile, no one was left to plow or sow" (al-Maqrīzī 1994: 42). Labor shortages are commonplace in the aftermath of mass mortality, but in Egypt, where the restoration of agricultural productivity necessitated rebuilding dikes and dredging clogged canals, a lack of manpower significantly hindered the country's resilience (Borsch 2005: 40–47; Scheidel 2017: 317–42). Readers who live in the United States and Europe and read this Element close to its date of publication may have benefitted from the unprecedented incentives and wages employers began to offer as the death toll from the coronavirus mounted. Such readers, of course, are also aware that inflation and other factors quickly undercut these gains.

---

[14] Thucydides reported much the same with regard to the Athenian plague in 430 BCE (Thucydides, *History* 2.53.2–3).

4.3 In Europe's Middle Ages, Elites Exaggerated Social Shifts in the Aftermath of Mass Mortality and Satirized Perceived Social Climbers

Careful revisionist work by economic historians has tempered the assessment that the aftermath of the Black Death represented a golden age for laborers. Although Europe's population may have been reduced by a third, and although demand for labor was indeed high, prices quickly spiked alongside wages. According to A. R. Bridbury, "With the arrival of the Black Death wages rose once more. Contemporary outcry prepares one for a truly spectacular rise. But the figures do not tell a story which is in any way consistent with the volume of the outcry or the circumstantial detail of the chronicled horror" (Bridbury 1973: 583). The fourteenth-century poet John Gower (Figure 20), for example, reacted indignantly to this perceived rise in the status of the working class. In *Mirour de l'omme*, he reminisced about the days before the Black Death, writing,

> The labourers of olden times were not accustomed to eat wheat bread; their bread was made of beans and of other corn, and their drink was water. Then cheese and milk were as a feast to them; rarely had they any other feast than this. Their clothing was plain grey. Then was the world of such folk well-ordered. (quoted in Hatcher 1994: 16)

Gower's sentiments were widely shared among his social class. Thus, governments throughout Europe issued ordinances to regulate wages, restrict the bargaining power of laborers and artisans, and legislate their access to "luxuries." Samuel Cohn explains,

> [T]hese new laws reflect elites' further anxieties about class . . . . [T]he laws alleged that laborers now 'demanded quality wines and meats beyond their station'. For these elites the world had suddenly been turned upside down: to quote a Florentine decree of 9 October 1348: 'while many citizens had suddenly become the poor, the poor had become rich'. The Florentine chronicler Stefani said much the same. (Cohn 2007: 480)

Regardless of whether elites' fear of plummeting from the top of the food chain to the bottom was realistic, the prospect deeply concerned many members of Europe's upper classes. In *Vox Clamantis*, Gower explored this theme at length. "[T]he fixed order of things is no more," he declared. " . . . The fox now protects the chickens, and the wolf the sheep . . . . Servants are now masters and masters are servants. . . . The peasant pretends to imitate the ways of the freeman, and gives the appearance of him in his clothes" (Gower 1962: 259).

Figure 20 John Gower depicted in an edition of *Vox Clamantis* and *Chronica Tripertita,* c. 1400 CE (Glasgow University Library MS Hunter 59 [T.2.17] folio 6 verso), public domain https://commons.wikimedia.org/wiki/File: John_Gower_world_Vox_Clamantis.jpg

To Gower, the peasants' ambitions were not only against the law but also against nature. Thus, the first book of *Vox Clamantis* relates a series of nightmares that together were meant to be interpreted as an allegorical prophecy of the Peasants' Revolt of 1381. In these pseudo-prophetic visions, peasants transform into donkeys who revolt and refuse to carry their accustomed loads. The asses develop airs, compulsively combing their manes to look as attractive as possible. Oxen refuse to plow and demand to be fed grain. Dogs desist from hunting game and contract mutually agreeable treaties with foxes, who then feel free to abandon their dens for the comfort of palaces. Cats, too, instead of catching rats, allow houses to become overrun with them (Gower 1962: 54–64). Finally, a jackdaw gathers the unruly animals together and launches into a speech, saying,

> O you low sort of wretches, which the world has subjugated for a long time by its law, look, now the day has come when the peasantry will triumph . . .. Let the law give over which used to hold us in check with its justice, and from here on let our court rule. (Gower 1962: 65)

Upon awakening, the narrator is deeply relieved to find the ox strapped to its yoke, the peasantry in bondage, the "villein" no longer warring, and the seed flourishing beneath plowed fields (Gower 1962: 94).

Elites have often mined the animal world for analogies useful in justifying their own power. The equation between beasts of burden and unfree laborers justifies inhumane labor practices, and the comparison with predator and prey legitimates violence. So too, in many cases the powerful present their social inferiors as vermin, fit for extermination if boundaries are transgressed (Bradley 2000; Bennett 2020). This point is pertinent for the argument mounted in this Element that the real and imagined social inversions taking place during famine were – in the course of the Egyptian New Year's Festival – dramatized through animal tales, in which the natural roles of the protagonists had been (temporarily) reversed. Such improbable scenarios served both to memorialize the destabilizations of hierarchy associated with famines and to provide a serious subject with a dash of fun. The meanings encoded in these tales were far from simple, however, and were audible to various members of their audience in very different registers.

4.4 The New Year's Festival Drew on Inversions for Laughter to Counterbalance Fear

Understanding the plot of the New Year's Festival is vital for comprehending the argument that follows. The period of solemnity preceding the festival coincides with the last five days of a seventy-day stretch during which the star Sirius disappears from sight. Mythologically, this star is understood as the sun god's daughter, conceptualized both as his solar eye and as a lioness who has stalked off to Nubia in anger. Enraged, she is the fierce side of many local goddesses. Her myth serves primarily, however, to explain a suite of natural phenomena that occur at the summer solstice, namely, why Sirius reappears after a long absence, the sun turns northward, the flood waters return, and the yearly plague abates (Richter 2016: 2–5).

The goddess's departure from Egypt leads the Nile to sink to its lowest levels and thereby threatens the survival of humankind. Out of care for his creations,

Figure 21 The Distant Goddess, as the Kushite Cat, listens to the "Jackal-ape," Dakka temple, Nubia, Creative Commons (photograph by Roland Unger) https://commons.wikimedia.org/wiki/File:DakkaTempleRomanChapel.jpg

the sun god dispatches the trickster god Thoth (or in some versions his son) in the form of a small baboon (or "Jackal-ape") to convince and cajole the goddess to return to Egypt (Figure 21). According to the early-second-century CE Demotic version of this myth, the Jackal-ape tries to persuade her by mounting a variety of arguments. He describes for her the misery and rampant crime that plague Egypt in her absence. He informs her that since she left, music, drunkenness, and laughter have ceased – implying perhaps that there may have been a moratorium on such activities for the five days prior to the advent of the New Year. The Jackal-ape also tempts the "Kushite Cat" with her favorite foods – foods eaten, perhaps, at the New Year's festival. He extolls the joys of home and tells her jokes to incline her heart to happiness. But one of his most successful tactics is stimulating the goddess's curiosity by narrating a series of didactic and diverting fables (Hoffmann and Quack 2007).

Mollified at last, the goddess turns toward home – with her flood waters and dancers in attendance – to rise as Sirius together with the sun on the dawn of the New Year at the advent of the summer solstice. As the Solar Eye, she turns north. On her return journey the goddess makes stops at each major temple, where she appears in the dead of night to her worshippers in the guise of the local goddess. As numerous sources attest, the celebrants aid the Jackal-ape in luring the goddess north by doing things known to please her, while awaiting her arrival in "porches of drunkenness." Not coincidentally, what pleased the goddess also pleased her worshippers: drinking spiked alcohol from festive containers, observing or participating in music and dance, and indulging in sexual relations. If the goddess had a mandate, it would have been that all the bodily desires of her worshippers *must* be satisfied to excess (Darnell 1995; von Lieven 2003; Jasnow and Smith 2010–2011; Bryan 2014: 100–23).

Various textual and archaeological sources from the Old and Middle Kingdoms demonstrate that versions of this myth enjoyed a long history in Egypt (Yoshimura, Kawai, and Kashiwagi 2005: 376–402; Horváth 2015: 131–41; Richter 2016: 2, n. 2). Most interesting for present purposes are the illustrations on two Ramesside ostraca (c. 1292–1077) of a fable narrated by the Jackal-ape in the Demotic version of the myth. It concerns an ill-fated arrangement between a cat and a vulture to babysit one another's children. On one ostracon a baboon faces a lion, as if engaged in dialogue, while above their heads a raptor with wings outstretched protects her eggs (Figure 22). In the other ostracon, a cat slinks away carrying both nest and nestlings on its back. Surmounting this scene is another relevant to the New Year's festival. An enthroned mouse converses with a cupbearer, who – judging from the caption – is either talking about cats or is a cat himself (Babcock 2022: 169; Figure 23).

Figure 22 The Kushite Cat listens to the baboon's fable about a raptor and her eggs (Ägyptisches Museum, Berlin Inv.-Nr. 21443), © bpk Bildagentur/ Ägyptisches Museum, Berlin /Art Resource, NY

Figure 23 Lower register: a cat makes off with the bird's eggs.
Upper register: an elite mouse converses with his cupbearer
(MFA 1976.784), © 2023 Museum of Fine Arts, Boston

That the ostraca depict episodes from stories told to children in the same manner as the Jackal-ape regaled the Kushite Cat is made clear by another ostracon (Babcock 2022: 94–8). On its top register a lion faces a baboon, as if listening to it, while in the register directly below a sidelocked youth mimics the Cat in paying rapt attention to another (Figure 24). Just as "before" and "after" scenes of the story of the raptor and the cat are depicted on different ostraca, the scene of the mouse and his cupbearer belongs to a narrative cycle known from other ostraca and papyri. Based on the reconstructed story cycle, the cupbearer is likely convincing the ambitious mouse to launch a war against cats. Events from the tale are illustrated on numerous ostraca and papyri – most, if not all, of which had been painted by artists who lived at the Theban workmen's village of Deir el-Medina (Brunner-Traut 1954; Flores 2004: 234–9; Babcock 2022: 69–70, 91–2).

The cupbearer's plan may be seen to come to fruition in the Turin "Erotic" Papyrus, a famously intriguing scroll in which animal fables share space with raucous sex scenes. In the latter, semi-bald votaries of Hathor have intercourse

Figure 24 The Kushite Cat and a boy listen to the baboon's fables
(Metropolitan Museum of Art 60.158), public domain www
.metmuseum.org/art/collection/search/545800?searchField=All&
sortBy=Relevance&ao=on&showOnly=openAccess&
amp;ft=60.158&offset=0&rpp=40&pos=1

with women adorned like cultic performers in an environment suffused with
Hathoric iconography (Figure 25).

Ann Roth and Jennifer Babcock, arguing from opposite ends of the
scroll, as it were, have separately suggested that the most likely explanation for this bizarre juxtaposition is that the papyrus would have been
commissioned as a New Year's votive gift for the goddess (Roth 2019;
Babcock 2022: 100). In the section of the papyrus showcasing animal
fables, King Mouse, in a chariot pulled by dogs, leads his mouse army in
storming a cat castle (Figure 26). The result of this war is that mice now
lord over cats. Cat servants tend to the needs of elite mice, fetching them
fancy food and drink, fanning them, grooming them, and even nursing
their children (Figure 27; Babcock 2022: 109–11, 113, 116–18, 121–3).

Figure 25 Turin Papyrus 55001, depicting things that please the goddess
(redrawn by Riva Weinstein after Omlin 1973: pl. 13)

Figure 26 Turin Papyrus 55001, animal scenes. Note the cat and mouse
war, the donkey dressed in fine linen, the crocodile playing a lute, the cat
herding birds, and the live mice bypassing the carcasses of cats
(redrawn by Riva Weinstein after Omlin 1973: pl. 13; inset of
restoration of cats and rats Omlin 1973: pl. 14)

That the tale of King Mouse endured for many centuries is demonstrated by
a portion of the decorative program of the Twenty-fifth-Dynasty chapel to the
God's Wife of Amun at Medamud (c. 700–650 BCE). Blocks depict jackal servants
preparing a banquet, a crocodile playing a lute, and an enthroned mouse attended
by a small cat servant (Figure 28). At Medamud, the Distant Goddess was closely
identified both with the God's Wife and the local goddess Rat-Tawy (Darnell 1995:
47; von Lieven 2009: 176–9). Thus, in a variant of the extant Demotic myth, the
Jackal-ape likely regaled the Kushite Cat with all the ways the world had gone
wrong when she left together with her flood waters: the poor became rich, good
shepherds turned bad, and her kinsmen – the cats – had been subjugated before
mere mice! This *last* argument, one suspects, proved his most compelling. As
Babcock has argued, the final scene in the story may have been illustrated on an
ostracon depicting a resplendent female cat – labeled "your daughter" – approach-
ing her (re)enthroned cat father (Figure 29; Babcock 2022: 92, 115).

Figure 27 A cat servant waits on an elite mouse at a feast (Brooklyn Museum 37.51E), Creative Commons (photograph by Gavin Ashworth) www.brooklynmuseum.org/opencollection/objects/3952

Figure 28 King Mouse and his cat servant on a block from a chapel to the God's Wife of Amun at Medamud, Twenty-fifth Dynasty (redrawn by Riva Weinstein after Omlin 1973: pl. 23b)

4.5 The Performances Offered Different Lessons for Different Audiences

At first glance, the absurdity of a tale of mice turning the tables on cats seems as simple as it is silly, but the fable may have gained potency from its polyvalence. According to theorists of humor, laughter often stems from incongruity,

Figure 29 Back on his throne, King Cat is approached by his daughter, perhaps an allusion to the pacified counterpart of the Kushite Cat (Louvre E32954), © Musée du Louvre, Dist. RMN-Grand Palais/Christian Décamps/Art Resource, NY

tensions that crave release, and feelings of superiority (Mitchell 1992a: 5–8). Illustrations of the New Year's fables hit each of these notes. The depictions of animals acting against their nature were funny, but the humor was made more edgy by the rigid class hierarchy the animals had violated. Just as Gower milked for comedic value his visions of donkeys insisting on fastidiously combed manes and foxes minding chickens, the Egyptian upper classes might snigger at the portrayal of the outsized ambitions of the recently poor when viewing King Mouse perched proudly on his throne, the donkey dressed in fine white linen in the Turin Papyrus, and the numerous scenes of prey under the care of "good" shepherds (Figure 26).

The creative mingling of fun and fright is the beating heart of a great many festivals that incorporate out-of-bounds behavior. Medieval and Ottoman narratives suggest that a world which rodents dominated had a correlate that was far scarier than it was funny. When the Nile was at its lowest ebb, as well as during times of famine, rodents almost invariably converged on settlements as active competitors with humans for the same scarce food. Unchecked, they consumed and destroyed the precious remnants of grain from storehouses as well as what remained in the fields (al-Baghdādī 1965: 63 *l*; Leitz 1994: 205–6; al-Maqrīzī 1994: 29; Sabra 2000: 155; Raphael 2013: 182; Mikhail 2017: 136–37,

176, 179). That such a serious famine-related threat underlay the fanciful tale is suggested – if the published restoration is to be trusted – by a vignette in the Turin Papyrus that depicts the carcasses of cats next to a scene of rodents heading unimpeded toward sheaves of wheat (Figure 26).

The narrative of King Mouse may have alarmed elites for many different reasons. Famine literature, prophecy, and ritual texts indicate that in times of extreme hunger the poor often *did* take up arms against the rich. Unlikely alliances – like those between mice and dogs in the Turin Papyrus – might well threaten the social order. The tale, then, almost certainly conveyed an additional message to the rich: should a true famine occur, elites would do well to share their food before real or fictive rats took it from them. The same mobs that assemble in protest outside bakeries, Egyptian history attests, often turn to storming government storehouses, the villas of the rich, or even the royal residence.

Festivals have often served to diffuse social tensions between the ruling class and those who labored for them. Such was the purpose, for example, of the festival license granted at Saturnalia and the celebrations between Christmas and New Year's in the antebellum South. During these holidays the enslaved and members of the lower classes were encouraged to cease work and drink heavily as a brief prelude to the return of forced labor (Bradley 1979). In his memoir, first published in 1845, Frederick Douglass discussed the utility of the Christmas holiday from the point of view of slaveholders:

> From what I know of the effect of these holidays upon the slave, I believe them to be among the most effective means in the hands of the slaveholder in keeping down the spirit of insurrection. Were the slaveholders at once to abandon this practice, I have not the slightest doubt it would lead to an immediate insurrection among the slaves. These holidays serve as con-ductors, or safety-valves, to carry off the rebellious spirit of enslaved humanity .... They do not give the slaves this time because they would not like to have their work during its continuance, but because they know it would be unsafe to deprive them of it. (Douglass 2009: 79–80)

According to Douglass, the freedom that masters granted enslaved people during the Christmas holiday came with an encouragement for them not only to indulge but to *over*indulge, until freedom became associated primarily with "a dose of vicious dissipation, artfully labeled with the name of liberty" (Douglass 2009: 80). "When the holidays ended," Douglass stated, "we staggered up from the filth of our wallowing, took a long breath, and marched to the field, – feeling, upon the whole, rather glad to go, from what our master had deceived us into a belief was freedom, back to the arms of slavery" (Douglass 2009: 80). These "slave holidays" and the Egyptian New Year's festival conform to Max Gluckman's category of "rituals of rebellion," in which real insurrections were forestalled by virtue of cathartic ritual enactments that occurred in a broadly sanctified carnival context that typically encouraged unbridled excess (Gluckman 1963: 127). Such sanctioned holidays promoted the message that a topsy-turvy world – admittedly fun for a short while – was neither healthy nor safe.

A custom of gift-giving at New Year's may also have been intended to prompt the poor to view the elite as generous rather than stingy. Amulets of the Kushite Cat, in her form of Sekhmet and Bastet, appear to have been given out on New Year's Day along with, perhaps, the New Year's flasks that are so abundant in the archaeological record (Pinch 1994: 39). One wonders, however, whether the custom of gift-giving might have been instituted in an attempt to anticipate Ipuwer's dystopia and avert it. With a gift, "he who could not weave for himself" would peaceably become "the owner of fine linen." A noble might give sweet myrrh to a man "who had no oil" and a mirror to a woman "who glimpsed her face in the water" in the hope that Egypt's lower classes, like the angry goddess, might be appeased (Enmarch 2008: 230). Such logic underlay the unusual generosity shown by Roman masters to their slaves at holidays (Bradley 1979: 113–15).

Ipuwer's speech before the Lord of All may offer partial substantiation for this theory in that it concludes with a list of things that are good, all of which may have occurred at the New Year's festival: drinking strong liquor, lords watching the rejoicing and being secure for the future, "when the need of every man is fulfilled with a blanket in the shade, and the door is closed on him who slept in a bush. Indeed it is good when fine linen is spread out on the day of the land's(?) festival"[15] (Enmarch 2008: 237–38). Finery for the children of nobles and linen for clothing, interestingly, are mentioned together in the Hymn to the Nile as beneficial things that vanish in times of famine (Lichtheim 1975: 208).

Traditionally, the transgressive chaos of carnival is acceptable to the elite precisely because the "freedom" granted is an exception to the rule. Certainly, the moral encoded into the frame story of King Mouse – like that of the *Prophecy of Neferti* – was that with the coming of the flood (incarnate in the Kushite Cat and a strong pharaoh), order would be restored. It is worth asking, however, what the tale of King Mouse did for the laboring classes in Egypt,

---

[15] The "land's festival" (*ḥb-t3*) has also been read "New Year" (*wpt-rnpt*) (Enmarch 2008: 200). If clothes were traditionally laid out for the poor at the New Year's festival, this might deepen our understanding of *Eloquent Peasant*. In the story, the peasant had been defrauded by a member of the elite who lay out clothing to block his path, such that the peasant's donkey stepped into a field of barley and consumed a mouthful. Instead of laying out the clothing to be generous to a member of the lower classes, then, the official had done so to exploit him.

who evidently enjoyed the holiday for their own reasons. Although festival license may be intended to serve as a safety-valve to prevent the frustrations of the oppressed from exploding in violent rebellion, these reversals encourage the lower classes to take liberties and to take "liberty" seriously (Connerton 1989: 50; Mitchell 1992b: 145–7, 154–8; Graeber and Wengrow 2021: 115–17).

Imaginative and temporary inversions, particularly if performed, typically offer members of the non-elite a rare opportunity to critique their social betters through "harmless" parody. Thus, stock characters are often imbued with distinctive mannerisms that make their true target (a local official perhaps) clearly identifiable (Mitchell 1992a: 21, 25; Counts and Counts 1992: 94–101; Sinavaiana 1992: 193, 195–6, 198, 211; Meskell 2004: 155, 166–7). Even if the Egyptian tales were only narrated by non-elites,[16] and not performed, the adventures of King Mouse drew attention to one of their own: to an individual who outwitted and outmaneuvered the class of predators that normally kept them firmly under paw. It may even have offered hope for the future. Just as the tale of King Mouse helped perpetuate the memory of famine by dramatizing the role reversals that often accompanied low Niles, its annual retelling – which, far more often than not, occurred when a strong pharaoh was in office – almost certainly helped the lower classes remember that efforts to revolt occasionally succeed.

The more subversive lessons encoded in the Egyptian New Year's festival have not lost their currency. In *The Caucasian Chalk Circle*, written in the immediate aftermath of World War II, Bertolt Brecht reframed Ipuwer's laments as an ode to revolution (Assmann 2003: 111–12). If the nobles lamented and the paupers were in glee, so much the better! So too, if he who had no grain now owned a granary, or if those who were forcibly confined could now go out without restraint. In a similar move, the contemporary Egyptian artist Alaa Awad memorialized King Mouse in street art that he painted through eyes that stung with tear gas during the events following the popular uprising against Hosni Mubarak (Morayef 2016: 200, 203; Figure 30). (In a world where "order" has been reimposed, the mural exists today only in photographs.)

At the tail end of 2022, as this Element neared its conclusion, the United Nations Security Council and the World Bank both issued warnings that a looming global food crisis is poised to cause social unrest and

---

[16] While the highest officials at Deir el-Medina could be considered elite, the village's nonmanagerial workers went on strike during food crises in the late Twentieth Dynasty and robbed tombs. Like Ipuwer's laundrymen and Gower's oxen, anger caused them to abandon their customary deference to the upper classes.

Figure 30 Egyptians posing next to an illustration of King Mouse, incorporated
by Alaa Awad into a mural after the popular revolt against Hosni Mubarak
(photograph courtesy of Alaa Awad)

famine.[17] At this time the West could do worse than to follow the
example of the priests who composed the Demotic version of the New
Year's myth. The fable of King Mouse – perhaps after the revolts and
famines of the early second century CE – seems to have been substituted
for a kinder, gentler variant. In the well-known Aesop's fable of the Lion
and the Mouse, which the Jackal-ape now tells the Kushite Cat, a mouse
chews through the ropes that bind a lion in gratitude for a kindness that
the lion had shown to it (Hoffmann and Quack 2007: 234-5). Unlike the
tale of King Mouse that we have been discussing, which stresses the
necessity of force in maintaining order, Aesop's tale, supposedly composed by an enslaved man and repeated by the Lord of Wisdom, offers
a different moral. It implies that what is *truly* good – on New Year's Day
and every day – is when lions and mice and people from all walks of life
act altruistically for the common good.

---

[17] See the press releases at Lack of Grain Exports Driving Global Hunger to Famine Levels, as War
in Ukraine Continues, Speakers Warn Security Council; World Bank Announces Planned
Actions for Global Food Crisis Response; and the 108 citations in 2022–2023 food crises –
Wikipedia.

References

Adamovich, A., and Granin, D. (1983). *A Book of the Blockade*. Moscow: Raduga.

Allen, J. P. (2002). *The Heqanakht Papyri*. New York: Metropolitan Museum of Art.

Allen, J. P. (2011). *The Debate between a Man and His Soul: A Masterpiece of Ancient Egyptian Literature*. Leiden: Brill.

Allen, J. P. (2015). *Middle Egyptian Literature: Eight Literary Works of the Middle Kingdom*. Cambridge: Cambridge University Press.

Arnold, D. (1988). *Famine: Social Crisis and Historical Change*. Oxford: Basil Blackwell.

Arz, H. W., Lamy, F., and Pätzold, J. (2006). A Pronounced Dry Event Recorded around 4.2 ka in Brine Sediments from the Northern Red Sea. *Quaternary Research*, **66**(3), 432–41.

Assmann, J. (2003). *The Mind of Egypt: History and Meaning in the Time of the Pharaohs*, trans. A. Jenkins. Cambridge, MA: Harvard University Press.

Assmann, J. (2006). *Religion and Cultural Memory*, trans. R. Livingstone. Stanford: Stanford University Press.

Aster, S. Z. (2015). Isaiah 19: The "Burden of Egypt" and Neo-Assyrian Imperial Policy. *Journal of the American Oriental Society*, **135**(3), 453–70.

Azeze, F. (1998). *Unheard Voices: Drought, Famine, and God in Ethiopian Oral Poetry*. Addis Ababa: Addis Ababa University Press.

Babcock, J. M. (2022). *Ancient Egyptian Animal Fables: Tree Climbing Hippos and Ennobled Mice*. Brill: Leiden.

al-Baghdādī, 'A. (1965) [1204]. *The Eastern Key*, trans. K. H. Zand, J. A. Videan and I. E. Videan. London: George Allen and Unwin.

Bazzana, G. B. (2018). The *Oracle of the Potter* and the "Apocalyptic Worldview" in Egypt. *Ephemerides Theologicae Lovanienses*, **94**(2), 207–22.

Bell, B. (1971). The Dark Ages in Ancient History. I. The First Dark Age in Egypt. *American Journal of Archaeology*, **75**(1), 1–26.

Bell, B. (1975). Climate and the History of Egypt: The Middle Kingdom. *American Journal of Archaeology*, **79**(3), 223–69.

Bennett, J. (2020). *Being Property Once Myself: Blackness and the End of Man*. Cambridge: Belknap Press of Harvard University Press.

Bernhardt, C. E., Horton, B. P., and Stanley, J.-D. (2012). Nile Delta Vegetation Response to Holocene Climate Variability. *Geology*, **40**(7), 615–18.

Beyerle, S. (2016). Authority and Propaganda – The Case of the Potter's Oracle. In J. Baden, H. Najman, and E. J. C. Tigchelaar, eds., *Sibyls, Scriptures, and Scrolls: John Collins at Seventy*. Leiden: Brill, pp. 167–84.

Blasius, A., and Schipper, B. U. (2002). Apokalyptik und Ägypten? – Erkenntnisse und Perspektiven. In A. Blasius and B. U. Schipper, eds., *Apokalyptik und Ägypten: eine kritische Analyse der relevanten Texte aus dem griechisch-römischen Ägypten*. Leuven: Peeters, pp. 277–302.

Blouin, K. (2014). *Triangular Landscapes: Environment, Society, and the State in the Nile Delta under Roman Rule*. Oxford: Oxford University Press.

Borghouts, J. F. (1978). *Ancient Egyptian Magical Texts*. Leiden: Brill.

Borsch, S. J. (2005). *The Black Death in Egypt and England. A Comparative Study*. Austin: University of Texas Press.

Bradley, K. R. (1979). Holidays for Slaves. *Symbolae Osloenses*, **54**, 111–18.

Bradley, K. (2000). Animalizing the Slave: The Truth of Fiction. *Journal of Roman Studies*, **90**, 110–25.

Bridbury, A. R. (1973). The Black Death. *Economic History Review*, **26**(4), 577–92.

Brunner-Traut, E. (1954). Der Katzenmäusekrieg im Alten und Neuen Orient. *Zeitschrift der Deutschen Morgenländischen Gesellschaft*, **104**(2), 347–51.

Bryan, B. (2014). Hatshepsut and Cultic Revelries in the New Kingdom. In J. M. Galán, B. M. Bryan, and P. F. Dorman, eds., *Creativity and Innovation in the Reign of Hatshepsut*. Chicago: Oriental Institute of the University of Chicago, pp. 93–123.

Butzer, K. W. (1997). Sociopolitical Discontinuity in the Near East c. 2200 B.C.E.: Scenarios from Palestine and Egypt. In H. N. Dalfes, G. Kukla, and H. Weiss, eds., *Third Millennium BC Climate Change and Old World Collapse*. Berlin: Springer-Verlag, pp. 245–96.

Butzer, K. W. (2012). Collapse, Environment, and Society. *PNAS*, **109**(10), 3632–39.

Caminos, R. A. (1954). *Late-Egyptian Miscellanies*. London: Oxford University Press.

Cohn, S. (2007). After the Black Death: Labour Legislation and Attitudes towards Labour in Late-Medieval Western Europe. *Economic History Review*, N.S., **60**(3), 457–85.

Collins, J. J. (1997). The Sibyl and the Potter: Political Propaganda in Ptolemaic Egypt. In J. J. Collins, ed., *Seers, Sybils and Sages in Hellenistic-Roman Judaism*. Leiden: Brill, pp. 199–210.

Connerton, P. (1989). *How Societies Remember*. Cambridge: Cambridge University Press.

Contardi, F. (2015). Disasters Connected with the Rhythm of the Nile in the Textual Sources. In G. C. Vittozzi, ed., *Egyptian Curses 2: A Research on Ancient Catastrophes*. Rome: Consiglio Nazionale delle Ricerche, Istituto di Studi sul Mediterraneo Antico, pp. 11–26.

Counts, D. R., and Counts, D. A. (1992). Exaggeration and Reversal: Clowning among the Lusi-Kaliai. In W. E. Mitchell, ed., *Clowning as Critical Practice: Performance Humor in the South Pacific*. Pittsburgh: University of Pittsburgh Press, pp. 88–103.

Creasman, P. P. (2020). A Compendium of Recent Evidence from Egypt and Sudan for Climate Change during the Pharaonic Period. In T. Schneider and C. L. Johnston, eds., *The Gift of the Nile? Ancient Egypt and the Environment*. Tucson: Egyptian Expedition, pp. 15–48.

Darnell, J. C. (1995). Hathor returns to Medamûd. *Studien zur Altägyptischen Kultur*, **22**, 47–94.

Demidchik, A. (2011). The Date of the "Teaching for Merikare." In Eleonora Efimovna Kormysheva, Eugenio Fantusati, Danièle Michaux-Colombot, eds., *Cultural Heritage of Egypt and Christian Orient 6: Egypt and Near Eastern Countries III mill. B.C.–1 mill. A.D.* Moscow: Institute of Oriental Studies, pp. 49–70.

Dikötter, F. (2010). Mao's Great Leap to Famine. *New York Times*, December 15. www.nytimes.com/2010/12/16/opinion/16iht-eddikotter16.html, accessed May 2, 2023.

Douglass, F. (2009) [1845]. *Narrative of the Life of Frederick Douglass, An American Slave, Written by Himself*. Cambridge: Belknap Press of Harvard University Press.

Drioton, E. (1943). Une représentation de la famine sur un bas-relief égyptien de la Ve dynastie. *Bulletin de l'Institut d'Ègypte*, **25**, 45–54.

Dunand, F. (1977). L'Oracle du Potier et la formation de l'apocalyptique en Égypte. In F. Raphaël, F. Dunand, J. G. Heintz et al., eds., *L'Apocalyptique*. Paris: Paul Geuthner, pp. 41–67.

Engdahl, H. (2002). Philomela's Tongue: Introductory Remarks on Witness Literature. In H. Engdahl, ed., *Witness Literature: Proceedings of the Nobel Centennial Symposium*. New Jersey: World Scientific, pp. 1–14.

Enmarch, R. (2008). *A World Upturned: Commentary on and Analysis of The Dialogue of Ipuwer and the Lord of All*. Oxford: Oxford University Press.

Escolano-Poveda, M. (2017). New Fragments of Papyrus Berlin 3024: The Missing Beginning of the Debate between a Man and His Ba and the Continuation of the Tale of the Herdsman (P. Mallorca I and II). *Zeitschrift für ägyptische Sprache und Altertumskunde*, **144**(1), 16–54.

Felber, H. (2002). Die Demotische Chronik. In A. Blasius and B. U. Schipper, eds., *Apokalyptik und Ägypten: eine kritische Analyse der relevanten Texte aus dem griechisch-römischen Ägypten.* Leuven: Peeters, pp. 65–111.

Flores, D. (2004). The Topsy-Turvy World. In G. N. Knoppers and A. Hirsch, eds., *Egypt, Israel, and the Ancient Mediterranean World: Studies in Honor of Donald B. Redford.* Leiden: Brill, pp. 233–55.

Forstner-Müller, I., Said, A. M., Rose, P. et al. (2019). First Report on the Town of Kom Ombo. *Jahreshefte des Österreichischen Archäologischen Institutes in Wien*, **88**, 57–92.

Frankfort, H. (1978). *Kingship and the Gods*, reprint. Chicago: University of Chicago Press.

Frankfurter, D. (1992). Lest Egypt's City Be Deserted: Religion and Ideology in the Egyptian Response to the Jewish Revolt (116–117 C.E.). *Journal of Jewish Studies*, **43**(2), 203–20.

Frankfurter, D. (1993). *Elijah in Upper Egypt: The Apocalypse of Elijah and Early Egyptian Christianity.* Minneapolis: Fortress Press.

Gee, J. (2015). Did the Old Kingdom Collapse? A New View of the First Intermediate Period. In P. Der Manuelian and T. Schneider, eds., *Towards a New History for the Egyptian Old Kingdom.* Leiden: Brill, pp. 60–75.

Ginzburg, L. (2016). *Notes from the Blockade*, trans. A. Myers, and *A Story of Pity and Cruelty*, trans. A. Livingstone. London: Vintage.

Gluckman, M. (1963). *Order and Rebellion in Tribal Africa.* London: Cohen & West.

Gnirs, A. M. (2006). Das Motiv des Bürgerkriegs in Merikare und Neferti – Zur Literatur der 18. Dynastie. In G. Moers et al., eds., *jn.t dr.w: Festschrift für Friedrich Junge*, vol. 1. Göttingen: Seminar für Ägyptologie und Koptologie, pp. 207–65.

Gnirs, A. M. (2015). Royal Power in Times of Disaster. In F. Coppens, J. Janák, and H. Vymazalová, eds., *Royal versus Divine Authority: Acquisition, Legitimization and Renewal of Power.* Wiesbaden: Harrassowitz, pp. 109–43.

Goldberg, A. (2017). *Trauma in the First Person: Diary Writing during the Holocaust*, trans. S. Sermoneta-Gertel and A. Greenberg. Bloomington: Indiana University Press.

Gower, J. (1962) [1381]. *The Major Latin Works of John Gower*, ed. E. W. Stockton. Seattle: University of Washington Press.

Graeber, D., and Wengrow, D. (2021). *The Dawn of Everything: A New History of Humanity.* New York: Farrar, Straus and Giroux.

Hagen, F. (2013). An Eighteenth Dynasty Writing Board (Ashmolean 1948.91) and The Hymn to the Nile. *Journal of the American Research Center in Egypt*, **49**, 73–91.

Hagen, F. (2019). New Copies of Old Classics: Early Manuscripts of Khakheperreseneb and the Instruction of a Man for His Son. *Journal of Egyptian Archaeology*, **105**(2), 177–208.

Hamdan, M., Hassan, F. A., Flower, R. J. et al. (2016). Climate and Collapse of Egyptian Old Kingdom: A Geoarchaeological Approach. In G. C. Vittozzi and F. Porcelli, eds., *Archaeology and Environment: Understanding the Past to Design the Future: A Multidisciplinary Approach*. Rome: Consiglio Nazionale delle Ricerche, Istituto di Studi sul Mediterraneo Antico, pp. 89–100.

Harper, K. (2017). *The Fate of Rome: Climate, Disease, and the End of an Empire*. Princeton: Princeton University Press.

Hassan, F. A. (1997). Nile Floods and Political Disorder in Early Egypt. In H. N. Dalfes, G. Kukla, and H. Weiss, eds., *Third Millennium BC Climate Change and Old World Collapse*. Berlin: Springer-Verlag, pp. 1–23.

Hassan, F. A. (2007). Droughts, Famine and the Collapse of the Old Kingdom: Re-Reading Ipuwer. In Z. Hawass and J. Richards, eds., *The Archaeology and Art of Ancient Egypt: Essays in Honor of David B. O'Connor*, vol. I. Cairo: Supreme Council of Antiquities, pp. 357–77.

Hassan, F. A., Hamdan, M. A., Flower, R. J. et al. (2017). Holocene Alluvial History and Archaeological Significance of the Nile Floodplain in the Saqqara-Memphis Region, Egypt. *Quaternary Science Reviews*, **176**, 51–70.

Hatcher, J. (1994). England in the Aftermath of the Black Death. *Past & Present*, **144**(1), 3–35.

Hawass, Z., and Verner, M. (1996). Newly Discovered Blocks from the Causeway of Sahure (Archaeological Report). *Mitteilungen des Deutschen Archäologischen Instituts Abteilung Kairo*, **52**, 177–86, pls. 54–56.

Henrichs, A. (1968). Vespasian's Visit to Alexandria. *Zeitschrift für Papyrologie und Epigraphik*, **3**, 51–80.

Hillard, T. (2010). The God Abandons Antony: Alexandrian Street Theatre in 30 BC. In A. Woods, A. McFarlane, and S. Binder, eds., *Egyptian Culture and Society: Studies in Honour of Naguib Kanawati*, vol I. Cairo: Supreme Council of Antiquities, pp. 201–17.

Hoffmann, F., and Quack, J. F. (2007). *Anthologie der demotischen Literatur*. Berlin: Lit.

Höflmayer, F. (2015). The Southern Levant, Egypt, and the 4.2 ka BP Event. In H. Meller, H. W. Arz, R. Jung und et al., eds., *2200 BC – A Climatic Breakdown as a Cause for the Collapse of the Old World?* Halle: Landesmuseums für Vorgeschichte, pp. 113–30.

Hornung, E., Krauss, R., and Warburton, D. A., eds. (2006). *Ancient Egyptian Chronology*. Leiden: Brill.

Horváth, Z. (2015). Hathor and her Festivals at Lahun. In G. Miniaci and W. Grajetzki, eds., *The World of Middle Kingdom Egypt (2000–1550 BC)*, vol. I. London: Golden House, pp. 125–44.

Jansen-Winkeln, K. (2017). Zur Datierung der mittelägyptischen Literatur. *Orientalia*, N.S., **86**(1), 107–34.

Jasnow, R., and Smith, M. (2010–2011). "As for Those Who have Called me Evil, Mut will call them Evil": Orgiastic Cultic Behaviour and its Critics in Ancient Egypt (PSI Inv. [provv.] D 114a + PSI Inv. 3056 verso). *Enchoria*, **32**, 9–53.

Kaiser, M. (2010). The Holocaust's Uneasy Relationship with Literature. *The Atlantic*, December 28. www.theatlantic.com/entertainment/archive/2010/12/the-holocausts-uneasy-relationship-with-literature/67998/, accessed May 2, 2023.

Kákosy, L. (1966). Prophecies of Ram Gods. *Acta Orientalia Academiae Scientiarum Hungaricae*, **19**(3), 341–58.

Kerkeslager, A. (1998). The Apology of the Potter: A Translation of the Potter's Oracle. In I. Shirun-Grumach, ed., *Jerusalem Studies in Egyptology*. Wiesbaden: Harrassowitz, pp. 67–79.

Kochina, E. (2014). *Blockade Diary: Under Siege in Leningrad, 1941–1942*, trans. S. C. Ramer. New York: Ardis.

Koenen, L. (1970). The Prophecies of a Potter: A Prophecy of World Renewal Becomes an Apocalypse. In D. H. Samuel, ed., *Proceedings of the Twelfth International Congress of Papyrology*. Toronto: A. M. Hakkert, pp. 249–54.

van der Kolk, B. A. (2015). *The Body Keeps the Score: Brain, Mind, and Body in the Healing of Trauma*. New York: Penguin Books.

Kuraszkiewicz, K. O. (2016). Architectural Innovations Influenced by Climatic Phenomena (4.2 ka Event) in the Late Old Kingdom (Saqqara, Egypt). *Studia Quaternaria*, **33**(1), 27–34.

LaCapra, D. (2014). *Writing History, Writing Trauma*. Baltimore: Johns Hopkins University Press.

Leitz, C. (1994). *Tagewählerei: Das Buch ḥȝt nḥḥ pḥ.wy ḏt und verwandte Texte*. Wiesbaden: Harrassowitz.

Levi, P. (1988). *The Drowned and the Saved*, trans. R. Rosenthal. New York: Simon and Schuster.

Levi, P. (2015). *The Complete Works of Primo Levi*, ed. A. Goldstein. New York: Liveright.

Levine, M. G. (2006). *The Belated Witness: Literature, Testimony, and the Question of Holocaust Survival*. Stanford: Stanford University Press.

Li, C., Miles, T., Shen, L. et al. (2018). Early-Life Exposure to Severe Famine and Subsequent Risk of Depressive Symptoms in Late Adulthood: The China

Health and Retirement Longitudinal Study. *The British Journal of Psychiatry*, **213**(4), 579–86.

Lichtheim, M. (1945). The Songs of the Harpers. *Journal of Near Eastern Studies*, **4**(3), 178–212.

Lichtheim, M. (1975). *Ancient Egyptian Literature, Vol. I: The Old and Middle Kingdoms*. Berkeley: University of California Press.

Lichtheim, M. (1980). *Ancient Egyptian Literature, Vol. III: The Late Period*. Berkeley: University of California Press.

Lichtheim, M. (1988). *Ancient Egyptian Autobiographies Chiefly of the Middle Kingdom: A Study and an Anthology*. Freiburg: Universitätsverlag Freiburg Schweiz.

von Lieven, A. (2003). Wein, Weib und Gesang – Rituale für die Gefährliche Göttin. In C. Metzner-Nebelsick, ed., *Rituale in der Vorgeschichte, Antike und Gegenwart*. Rahden: Verlag Marie Leidorf, pp. 47–55.

von Lieven, A. (2009). Fragments of a Monumental Proto-Myth of the Sun's Eye. In G. Widmer and D. Devauchelle, eds., *Actes du IXe congrès international des études démotiques*. Cairo: Institut Français d'Archéologie Orientale, pp. 173–81.

Luria, S. (1929). Die Ersten werden die Letzten sein (Zur "sozialen Revolution" im Altertum). *Klio*, **22**, 405–31.

Manning, J. G. (2018). *The Open Sea: The Economic Life of the Ancient Mediterranean World from the Iron Age to the Rise of Rome*. Princeton: Princeton University Press.

Manning, S. W., Dee, M. W., Wild, E. M. et al. (2014). High-Precision Dendro-[14]C Dating of Two Cedar Wood Sequences from First Intermediate Period and Middle Kingdom Egypt and a Small Regional Climate-Related [14]C Divergence. *Journal of Archaeological Science*, **46**, 401–16.

al-Maqrīzī, A. (1994) [1405]. *Mamluk Economics: A Study and Translation of al-Maqrīzī's Ighāthah*, trans. A. Allouche. Salt Lake City: University of Utah Press.

Marks, L., Salem, A., Welc, F. et al. (2017). Holocene Lake Sediments from the Faiyum Oasis in Egypt: A Record of Environmental and Climate Change. *Boreas: An International Journal of Quaternary Research*, **47**(1), 62–79.

Marshall, M. H., Lamb, H. F., Huws, D. et al. (2011). Late Pleistocene and Holocene Drought Events at Lake Tana, the Source of the Blue Nile. *Global and Planetary Change*, **78**, 147–61.

McConnell, J. R., Sigl, M., Plunkett, G. et al. (2020). Extreme Climate after Massive Eruption of Alaska's Okmok Volcano in 43 BCE and Effects on the Late Roman Republic and Ptolemaic Kingdom. *PNAS*, **117**(27), 15443–9.

McGlothlin, E. (2006). *Second-Generation Holocaust Literature: Legacies of Survival and Perpetration*. Rochester: Camden House.

Meskell, L. (2004). *Object Worlds in Ancient Egypt: Material Biographies Past and Present*. Oxford: Berg.

Mikhail, A. (2008). The Nature of Plague in Late Eighteenth-Century Egypt. *Bulletin of the History of Medicine*, **82**(2), 249–75.

Mikhail, A. (2011). *Nature and Empire in Ottoman Egypt: An Environmental History*. Cambridge: Cambridge University Press.

Mikhail, A. (2017). *Under Osman's Tree: The Ottoman Empire, Egypt, and Environmental History*. Chicago: University of Chicago Press.

Mitchell, W. E. (1992a). Introduction: Mother Folly in the Islands. In W. E. Mitchell, ed., *Clowning as Critical Practice: Performance Humor in the South Pacific*. Pittsburgh: University of Pittsburgh Press, pp. 3–57.

Mitchell, W. E. (1992b). Horrific Humor and Festal Farce: Carnival Clowning in Wape Society. In W. E. Mitchell, ed., *Clowning as Critical Practice: Performance Humor in the South Pacific*. Pittsburgh: University of Pittsburgh Press, pp. 145–66.

Modrzejewski, J. M. (1997). *The Jews of Egypt from Rameses II to Emperor Hadrian*, trans. R. Cornman. Princeton: Princeton University Press.

de Montholon, C. (1847). *History of the Captivity of Napoleon at St. Helena*, vol. IV. London: Henry Colburn.

Morayef, S. (2016). Pharaonic Street Art: The Challenge of Translation. In M. Baker, ed., *Translating Dissent: Voices from and with the Egyptian Revolution*. New York: Routledge, pp. 194–207.

Moreno García, J. C. (1997). *Études sur l'administration, le pouvoir et l'idéologie en Égypte, de l'Ancien au Moyen Empire*. Liège: Centre Informatique de Philosophie et Lettres.

Moreno García, J. C. (2015). Climatic Change or Sociopolitical Transformation? Reassessing Late 3rd Millennium BC in Egypt. In H. Meller, H. W. Arz, R. Jung et al., eds., *2200 BC – A Climatic Breakdown as a Cause for the Collapse of the Old World?* Halle: Landesmuseums für Vorgeschichte, pp. 79–96.

Morenz, L. D. (1999). Geschichte als Literatur. Reflexe der Ersten Zwischenzeit in den *Mahnworten*. In J. Assmann and E. Blumenthal, eds., *Literatur und Politik im pharaonischen und ptolemäischen Ägypten*. Cairo: Institut Français d'Archéologie Orientale, pp. 111–38.

Morenz, L. D. (2010). Der existentielle Vorwurf – an wen ist er adressiert? Überlegungen anläßlich einer Neubearbeitung der Admonitions. *Lingua Aegyptia*, **18**, 263–7.

Morris, E. (2006). "Lo, Nobles Lament, The Poor Rejoice": State Formation in the Wake of Social Flux. In G. M. Schwartz and J. J. Nichols, eds., *After Collapse: The Regeneration of Complex Societies*. Tucson: University of Arizona Press, pp. 58–71.

Morris, E. (2019). Ancient Egyptian Exceptionalism: Fragility, Flexibility and the Art of Not Collapsing. In N. Yoffee, ed., *The Evolution of Fragility: Setting the Terms*. Cambridge: McDonald Institute for Archaeological Research, pp. 61–87.

Morris, E. (2020). Writing Trauma: Ipuwer and the Curation of Cultural Memory. In R. E. Averbeck and K. L., Younger Jr., eds., *"An Excellent Fortress for His Armies, a Refuge for the People": Egyptological, Archaeological, and Biblical Studies in Honor of James K. Hoffmeier*. University Park: Penn State University Press/Eisenbrauns, pp. 231–52.

Morris, E. (2022). Reassessing the Value of Autobiographical Inscriptions from the First Intermediate Period and "Pessimistic Literature" for Understanding Egypt's Social History. In D. Candelora, N. Ben-Marzouk, and K. M. Cooney, eds., *Ancient Egyptian Society: Challenging Assumptions, Exploring Approaches*. New York: Routledge, pp. 265–78.

Ó Gráda, C. (2001). Famine, Trauma and Memory. *Béaloideas*, **69**, 121–43.

Ó Gráda, C. (2009). *Famine: A Short History*. Princeton: Princeton University Press.

Ó Gráda, C. (2015). Eating People is Wrong, and Other Essays on Famine, Its Past, and Its Future. Princeton: Princeton University Press.

Omlin, J. A. (1973). *Der Papyrus 55001 und seine satirisch-erotischen Zeichnungen und Inschriften*. Turin: Edizioni d'arte fratelli Pozzo.

Parkinson, R. B. (2002). *Poetry and Culture in Middle Kingdom Egypt: A Dark Side to Perfection*. New York: Continuum.

Peet, T. E. (1930). *The Great Tomb-Robberies of the Twentieth Egyptian Dynasty. I: Text*. Oxford: Clarendon Press.

Peri, A. (2017). *The War within: Diaries from the Siege of Leningrad*. Cambridge, MA: Harvard University Press.

von Pilgrim, C. (1999). Der Tempel des Jahwe. *MDAIK*, **55**, 142–5.

Pinch, G. (1994). *Magic in Ancient Egypt*. London: British Museum Press.

Pleysier, A. (2008). *Frozen Tears: The Blockade and Battle of Leningrad*. New York: University Press of America.

Porten, B. (1968). *Archives from Elephantine: The Life of an Ancient Jewish Military Colony*. Berkeley: University of California Press.

Quack, J. F. (1992). *Studien zur Lehre für Merikare*. Wiesbaden: Harrassowitz.

Quack, J. F. (2002). Ein neuer prophetischer Text aus Tebtynis. In A. Blasius and B. U. Schipper, eds., *Apokalyptik und Ägypten: eine kritische Analyse der relevanten Texte aus dem griechisch-römischen Ägypten*. Leuven: Peeters, pp. 253–74.

Quack, J. F. (2012). Danaergeschenk des Nil? Zu viel oder zu wenig Wasser im Alten Ägypten. In A. Berlejung, ed., *Disaster and Relief Management*. Tübingen: Mohr Siebeck, pp. 333–81.

Quack, J. F. (2016). Prophetische und apokalyptische Texte aus dem späten Ägypten. In K. Martin and C. Sieg, eds., *Zukunftsvisionen zwischen Apokalypse und Utopie*. Würzburg: Ergon, pp. 83–106.

Quack, J. F. (2021). Patros. *Das wissenschaftliche Bibellexikon im Internet (WiBiLex)*, www.bibelwissenschaft.de/stichwort/30591/, accessed January 5, 2023.

Raphael, S. K. (2013). *Climate and Political Climate: Environmental Disasters in the Medieval Levant*. Leiden: Brill.

Rea, J. (1966). 2554. Predictions by Astrology. In J. W. B. Barns, P. J. Parsons, E. G. Turner, eds., *The Oxyrhynchus Papyri Part XXXI*. London: Egypt Exploration Fund, pp. 77–83.

Redford, D. B. (2010). *City of the Ram-Man: The Story of Ancient Mendes*. Princeton: Princeton University Press.

Richter, B. A. (2016). *The Theology of Hathor of Dendera: Aural and Visual Scribal Techniques in the Per-Wer Sanctuary*. Atlanta: Lockwood Press.

Rosenberg, S. G. (2004). The Jewish Temple at Elephantine. *Near Eastern Archaeology*, **67**(1), 4–13.

Roth, A. M. (2019). The Audience for Ancient Egyptian Erotic Art. Paper presentation at *12th International Congress of Egyptologists*, Cairo, November 3–8.

Sabra, A. (2000). *Poverty and Charity in Medieval Islam: Mamluk Egypt, 1250–1517*. Cambridge: Cambridge University Press.

Scheidel, W. (2017). *The Great Leveler: Violence and the History of Inequality from the Stone Age to the Twenty-First Century*. Princeton: Princeton University Press.

Schipper, B. U. (2014). "The City by the Sea will be a Drying Place": Isaiah 19.1–25 in Light of Prophetic Texts from Ptolemaic Egypt. In N. MacDonald and K. Brown, eds., *Monotheism in Late Prophetic and Early Apocalyptic Literature*. Tübingen: Mohr Siebeck, pp. 25–56.

Schneider, T. (2017). "What Is the Past but a Once Material Existence Now Silenced?": The First Intermediate Period from an Epistemological Perspective. In F. Höflmayer, ed., *The Late Third Millennium in the Ancient Near East: Chronology, C14, and Climate Change*. Chicago: Oriental Institute of the University of Chicago, pp. 311–22.

Seidlmayer, S. (2000). The First Intermediate Period (c.2160–2055 BC). In I. Shaw, ed., *The Oxford History of Ancient Egypt*. New York: Oxford University Press, pp. 118–47.

Seidlmayer, S. J. (2001). *Historische und moderne Nilstände. Untersuchungen zu den Pegelablesungen des Nils von der Frühzeit bis in die Gegenwart.* Berlin: Achet Verlag.

Simpson, W. K. (1991). The Political Background of the Eloquent Peasant. *Göttinger Miszellen*, **120**, 95–9.

Simpson, W. K. (1996). *Belles Lettres* and Propaganda. In A. Loprieno, ed., *Ancient Egyptian Literature: History and Forms*. Leiden: Brill, pp. 435–43.

Simpson, W. K. (2001). Studies in the Twelfth Egyptian Dynasty III: Year 25 in the Era of the Oryx Nome and the Famine Years in Early Dynasty 12. *Journal of the American Research Center in Egypt*, **38**, 7–8.

Simpson, W. K. (2003). *The Literature of Ancient Egypt: An Anthology of Stories, Instructions, Stelae, Autobiographies, and Poetry*, 3rd ed. New Haven: Yale University Press.

Sinavaiana, C. (1992). Where the Spirits Laugh Last: Comic Theater in Samoa. In W. E. Mitchell, ed., *Clowning as Critical Practice: Performance Humor in the South Pacific*. Pittsburgh: University of Pittsburgh Press, pp. 192–218.

Soukiassian, G. (1997). A Governor's Palace at 'Ayn Asil, Dakhla Oasis. *Egyptian Archaeology*, **11**, 15–17.

Stauder, A. (2013). *Linguistic Dating of Middle Egyptian Literary Texts*. Hamburg: Widmaier.

Stein, A., F. H. Pierik, G. H. W. Verrips et al. (2009). Maternal Exposure to the Dutch Famine before Conception and during Pregnancy: Quality of Life and Depressive Symptoms in Adult Offspring. *Epidemiology*, **20**(6), 909–15.

Thériault, C. A. (1993). The Instruction of Amenemhat as Propaganda. *Journal of the American Research Center in Egypt*, **30**, 151–60.

Thissen, H.-J. (2002). Das Lamm des Bokchoris. In A. Blasius and B. U. Schipper, eds., *Apokalyptik und Ägypten: eine kritische Analyse der relevanten Texte aus dem griechisch-römischen Ägypten*. Leuven: Peeters, pp. 113–38.

Tuchman, B. W. (1978). *A Distant Mirror: The Calamitous 14th Century*. New York: Ballantine Books.

Vandier, J. (1936). *La famine dans l'Égypte ancienne*. Cairo: Institut Français d'Archéologie Orientale.

Welc, F., and Marks, L. (2014). Climate Change at the End of the Old Kingdom in Egypt around 4200 BP: New Geoarchaeological Evidence. *Quaternary International*, **324**, 124–33.

Wiesel, E. (1965). Everybody's Victim. *New York Times*, October 31. www .nytimes.com/1965/10/31/archives/everybodys-victim-the-painted-bird-by-jerry-kosinski-272-pp-boston.html, accessed May 2, 2023.

Yang, J. (2008). *Tombstone: The Great Chinese Famine, 1958–1962*, trans. S. Mosher and J. Guo. New York: Farrar, Straus and Giroux.

Yoshimura, S., Kawai, N., and Kashiwagi, H. (2005). A Sacred Hillside at Northwest Saqqara: A Preliminary Report on the Excavations 2001–2003. *Mitteilungen des Deutschen Archäologischen Instituts Abteilung Kairo*, **61**, 361–402.

Zandee, J. (1992). *Der Amunhymnus des Papyrus Leiden I 344, Verso*, vol. 2. Leiden: Rijksmuseum van Oudheden.

Zhao, X., Liu, Y., Salem, A. et al. (2017). Migration of the Intertropical Convergence Zone in North Africa during the Holocene: Evidence from Variations in Quartz Grain Roundness in the Lower Nile Valley, Egypt. *Quaternary International*, **449**(3), 22–8.

Acknowledgments

Dedicated with gratitude to David, Wendy, and Dee for their sharp eyes, sage advice, and long-term love. Dedicated also to friends and family who have been patient while I've tried, in vain, to succinctly explain the central argument of the book. For image permissions, I am especially grateful to Steve Harvey, Zahi Hawass, and Daniel Warne. Finally, many thanks are due to the Lodge Fund, Gianluca Miniaci, Juan Carlos Moreno Garcia, Anna Stevens, Andrew Miller, Riva Weinstein, the anonymous reviewers, Sev, Jules, and a great many colleagues whose work I admire.

Cambridge Elements ⹀

Ancient Egypt in Context

Gianluca Miniaci

University of Pisa

Gianluca Miniaci is Associate Professor in Egyptology at the University of Pisa, Honorary Researcher at the Institute of Archaeology, UCL – London, and Chercheur associé at the École Pratique des Hautes Études, Paris. He is currently co-director of the archaeological mission at Zawyet Sultan (Menya, Egypt). His main research interest focuses on the social history and the dynamics of material culture in the Middle Bronze Age Egypt and its interconnections between the Levant, Aegean, and Nubia.

Juan Carlos Moreno García

CNRS, Paris

Juan Carlos Moreno García (PhD in Egyptology, 1995) is a CNRS senior researcher at the University of Paris IV-Sorbonne, as well as lecturer on social and economic history of ancient Egypt at the École des Hautes Études en Sciences Sociales (EHESS) in Paris. He has published extensively on the administration, socio-economic history, and landscape organization of ancient Egypt, usually in a comparative perspective with other civilizations of the ancient world, and has organized several conferences on these topics.

Anna Stevens

University of Cambridge and Monash University

Anna Stevens is a research archaeologist with a particular interest in how material culture and urban space can shed light on the lives of the non-elite in ancient Egypt. She is Senior Research Associate at the McDonald Institute for Archaeological Research and Assistant Director of the Amarna Project (both University of Cambridge).

About the Series

The aim of this Elements series is to offer authoritative but accessible overviews of foundational and emerging topics in the study of ancient Egypt, along with comparative analyses, translated into a language comprehensible to non-specialists. Its authors will take a step back and connect ancient Egypt to the world around, bringing ancient Egypt to the attention of the broader humanities community and leading Egyptology in new directions.

Cambridge Elements ☰

Ancient Egypt in Context

Elements in the Series

A full series listing is available at: www.cambridge.org/AECE

Printed in the United States
by Baker & Taylor Publisher Services